The Organized Teacher's Guide to

Your First Year of Teaching

Steve Springer, M.A., Brandy Alexander, M.F.A., and Kimberly Persiani-Becker, Ed.D.

New York Chicago San Francisco Lisbon London Madrid Mexico City
Milan New Delhi San Juan Seoul Singapore Sydney Toronto

1 2 3 4 5 6 7 8 9 10 11 12 13 14 15   WFR/WFR   1 9 8 7 6 5 4 3 2 1 0

ISBN   978-0-07-174071-5 (book and CD set)
MHID   0-07-174071-6

ISBN   978-0-07-174069-2 (book alone)
MHID   0-07-174069-4

Library of Congress Control Number   2009942867

Interior design by Village Bookworks, Inc.

Interior and cover illustrations by Steve Springer

McGraw-Hill books are available at special quantity discounts to use as premiums and sales promotions or for use in corporate training programs. To contact a representative, please e-mail us at bulksales@mcgraw-hill.com.

This book is printed on acid-free paper.

CONTENTS

NORTH
Focal Point

page 1

SOUTH
Teacher's Space

page 47

Contents   iv

EAST
Student Space

page 83

Contents

WEST
Student and Teacher Space

page 114

Contents   vi

AERIAL VIEW
Looking Down from Above

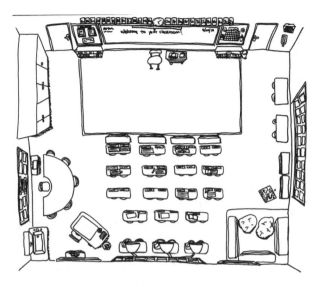

page 145

Contents

WELCOME, NEW TEACHER!

Welcome to the beginning of your teaching career! You are in for an amazing experience, one that is a tremendous privilege. We will help you begin your journey, so that you develop your skills over time with as little stress and as few mistakes as possible. A good start is critical.

Your role as teacher is a powerful one. Parents entrust you with the most important part of their lives: their children. It is your job to nurture, educate, and support students' social and intellectual growth.

You are not just their teacher—at times you will be their nurse, their counselor, their parent, their friend, their disciplinarian, and their biggest cheerleader. Your students will become your family, and so there will be tough times, moments when you laugh together, and moments when you are upset with one another.

You may need the support of a buddy teacher, a staff member, an administrator, and/or the parents.

We hope the ideas and experiences that we share in this book will support you as you firmly plant your feet and get off to a great start.

Good luck! *We're rooting for you.*

A NOTE TO THE TEACHER

 This CD icon is used in the text margin of this book to direct you to a template on the accompanying CD that relates to the text.

NORTH
Focal Point

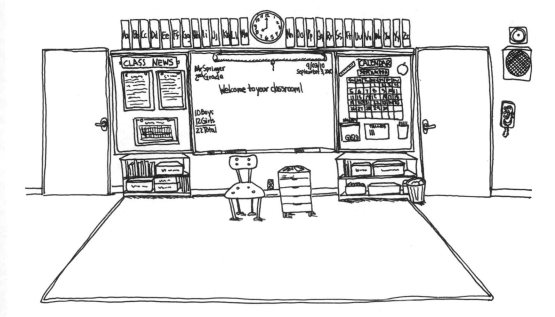

The North side of the room is the focal point for the entire class. This is the front of the classroom, where a lot of things happen. Students usually enter and exit from this part of the classroom, and attention is most often drawn here throughout the day. You nearly always find the whiteboard or chalkboard, the maps, and the projector here. It's where the teacher's delivery of whole class instruction takes place. In short, this is where the tone of the classroom is set.

In this section, we cover all the critical activity that takes place at the focal point—everything from classroom organization and setup to whole class instruction and management techniques.

Look for help with the following:

Beginning of the Year Checklists

Being prepared for your first day of class is the key to a successful start to your school year. There is so much to set up and prepare for! Once the students enter your classroom and the school year gets started, it's hard to find the time for this kind of preparation. Following are some ideas that you will want to have in place. Not all of the items will be necessary, depending on your school or grade level, but you'll want to be as ready as you can be before your students come into the classroom.

26
First Day
Classroom
Checklist

Classroom Environment

Desk Arrangement

Your desk arrangement should facilitate learning and smooth transitions throughout the room.

CONSIDERATIONS

- Position desks so that all students have equal access to the front of the classroom (posted alphabet, number lines, etc.).
- Have an extra desk or two available, in case additional students are temporarily assigned to your classroom.
- Make the arrangement work for you and your teaching style.
- Work with an arrangement that facilitates cooperative learning groups, if possible.

Teacher's Desk

Place your desk in a location where you have an optimal view of the entire classroom and where you feel most comfortable working.

CONSIDERATIONS

- Locate your desk near the intercom or phone for easy access.
- Be sure your desk is near a power outlet and, if one is available, an Internet connection.
- Place your desk in an area with low traffic (away from the sink and pencil sharpener, for example).

School Binder

It is helpful to have a binder that contains procedures and policies about your school and district. This may be provided for you; if not, you should create your own. Procedures and policies are updated from time to time, and having a place to keep all your hard copies is important.

- Keep the binder in an easily accessible place.
- Update pages as you receive them.

Hall Passes

Hall passes are proof that a student has received permission to leave his or her classroom.

32
Hall Passes

CONSiDERATiONS

- Color, cut, and glue the pass to cardstock, or laminate it if using a lighter weight paper.
- Create passes for specific destinations (for example, a Nurse pass and an Office pass).

Welcome Sign

A welcome sign (perhaps attached to a yardstick to hold for easy viewing) can assist you in picking your students up for the first time, or it can make your classroom easier to find.

CONSiDERATiONS

- Use large, easy-to-read print.
- Make your welcome sign friendly and welcoming.
- Include the teacher's name, room number, and grade level.

Bulletin Boards

Bulletin boards create an important first impression of your classroom. They showcase your students' work, and you will want them to last as long as possible. Because you will be changing your students' displayed work often, the bulletin boards need to be able to handle these changes.

CONSiDERATiONS

- Use a durable, fadeless paper for your background. Many teacher supply stores sell this, and it is well worth the investment.
- Choose a color that you like and that is pleasing to the eye.
- Select borders that coordinate with the background color. It is often possible to use a border that relates to a current theme of study.
- Keep bulletin boards symmetrical and well organized.
- Use an appropriate title, include a question to invite interaction, and provide the rubric for student work displayed.
- Designate one bulletin board for each subject.

Calendar

The calendar can be a powerful learning tool and can be used to create practical applications of learned math skills.

- Place the calendar in full view in the front of the room.
- Keep a clear path to the calendar for easy interaction and instruction.
- Keep materials that will be used with the calendar organized and nearby (for example, toy money, names of the week, tens and ones sticks).
- Use seasonal or monthly themes for the calendar.

Teacher Tools

Keep your instructional materials organized, and store them close to where they are used. If you use an overhead projector, have your pens, paper towels, manipulatives, and other related materials close by. Consider a desk or a small drawer storage bin on wheels that can be positioned in the area where you deliver most of your instruction.

- Organize all necessary materials in advance.
- Keep everything in its place; after using any instructional material, put it back.

Closet

An organized closet means easy access to your materials and supplies. As the year progresses, things can get hectic, so starting off with and maintaining an organized closet can help keep your class on track.

- Create an organizing system that works well for you.
- Place frequently used items on the most accessible shelves, usually the center of the closet rather than the top or bottom shelves.
- Train students to remove and return items neatly.
- Use labels so that items are easy to find.

Learning Centers

Learning centers are hands-on extensions of learning. They are set up around the room to be accessed during designated times.

- Keep learning centers simple. Try one or two learning centers at first, and add more when you are ready.
- Label each learning center.

- Introduce each learning center to the class before the students use it. Students will benefit more from their time spent at the learning center if they understand the expectations from the very beginning.
- Select activities that can be completed independently.
- Establish rules and guidelines for each learning center (for example, work in only one center at a time, only two students work at a center at a time).

Library

The classroom library is a place where students can go to read about, explore, and research what they are learning in class.

CONSIDERATIONS

- Organize books in tubs for lower grades or on shelves for upper grades.
- Categorize books according to subject, theme, or genre.
- Establish a simple checkout system.
- Make the library a comfortable area. Beanbag chairs make for comfortable seating.

51
Library
Sign-Out Sheet

Games

Having board games and puzzles available to students provides opportunities for them to work and play collaboratively. These materials challenge students' higher-level thinking skills, and having them in the classroom makes it possible for you to have some students work in small groups while others are occupied with the games.

CONSIDERATIONS

- Keep games organized in a designated area.
- Always introduce games before making them available.
- Introduce only one game a week so that students clearly understand the rules.
- Have students work toward earning a new game (for example, 30 points of good behavior during the week will earn a new game for the class).
- Yard sales are a great place to find games and puzzles.
- Students could donate old games or puzzles to your classroom, if they have their parent's permission.

Computers

Significant use of computers is a must in today's classrooms. Whenever possible, incorporate computer activities into your classroom and daily schedule.

16
Computer
Sign-In Sheet

- Position computers close to an outlet and Internet access, but where they will not be a distraction for students involved in other activities.
- Establish rules and a system of rotation.
- Demonstrate your expectations and rules for use.

17
Computer User
Name and
Password Log

Learning Tools

Learning tools include materials that students might have on their desktops or in a designated location. Having them readily available provides students with tools and resources for learning, as well as allowing smoother transitions.

CONSiDERATiONS

- Appoint a designated class monitor to pass out and collect materials.
- Establish rules stating when items can be used.
- Introduce each item and its purpose.

Board

The chalkboard or whiteboard is usually the focal point of the classroom. It is generally what students see first when they enter the classroom. Keep it clean and well organized.

CONSiDERATiONS

- Set up the room to face the board that you will be using most.
- Get supplies for the board (for example, chalk, eraser, markers, spray cleaner), and keep them in a designated spot nearby.
- Update the board daily with information such as the date, teacher's name, daily agenda, daily standards, and daily student count (boys, girls, total).

Technology

Educational technology is more readily available to the classroom teacher now than ever before. This equipment and the capabilities it offers can help make the presentation of lessons and reports easier and more effective.

23
Equipment
Inventory

CONSiDERATiONS

- Locate equipment close to power outlets.
- Keep equipment in good working order.
- Maintain an adequate supply of markers, paper towels, and extra bulbs.
- Test all equipment before using it.
- Train student monitors to set up and take down equipment.
- Always store equipment in a secure place.

Rules

Classroom rules set the tone and establish boundaries in the classroom. Developing them together with your students can be a very powerful experience for the group. A basic set of rules can be posted initially and adapted later for a particular class.

CONSIDERATIONS

- Keep rules short and sweet. Three to five rules should be enough.
- Use a positive perspective: Try "Keep your hands and feet to yourself" rather than "Don't hit."
- Be consistent once rules are established.
- Set clear consequences for infractions.

Schedule

A class schedule establishes a routine and provides structure, which is one of the most powerful aspects of a well-run classroom.

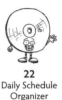

22
Daily Schedule
Organizer

CONSIDERATIONS

- Ask to see the schedules of fellow grade-level teachers.
- Find a schedule that works for you.
- Be flexible. There will be days with interruptions—from assemblies to fire drills. Go with the flow, and know that you may not get to everything every day.

Behavior

Behavior management can be a challenge, depending on the class. Clear expectations, consistency, and follow-through are the keys to success. Keeping behavior logs and incorporating behavior contracts into your classroom management can help track behavior. These records provide important information when preparing for conferences, assigning grades, and preparing progress reports throughout the year.

06
Behavior
Contract
07
Behavior Log
08
Behavior
Notification
47
Incident
Behavior Log

CONSIDERATIONS

- Determine appropriate rewards for the behavior management system for your classroom.
- Gather all materials, such as index cards, stickers, and stamps.
- Follow through with stated rewards and punishments.
- Be consistent.
- Incorporate behavior contracts into your classroom management.
- Use behavior logs to track students' behavior.
- Inform students and parents of your behavior management system.

Focal Point

Students

If you have materials that your students will need on a routine basis ready and organized before the beginning of the school year, your job will be considerably easier. Be prepared with extra supplies. Once the school year begins, student monitors can be in charge of these classroom materials.

Name Tags and Name Plates

27
First Day
Student
Checklist

Name tags are a good idea for the first day of school, regardless of the grade level you teach. Lower grade students' name tags can be worn around the neck while inside (but not while playing outside, because of safety hazards). Upper grade students can use adhesive or clip-on name tags. Name tags should be easy to read, especially for lower grade students.

Additionally, name plates can be attached to desks. Most schools have desk name plates that can be used, and teacher supply stores have name plates that can be purchased. For students in the lower grades, name plates not only give students a sense of place, but also provide a model for their name.

CONSIDERATIONS

- Keep the name tags simple. If they are too decorative, they are hard to read.
- Consider folding the name plates so that the bottom section forms a base and they can stand on the desks. This makes them easier to read.
- Have older students write their own names on their name tags and/or name plates.

Writing and Coloring Utensils

Included here are pencils, crayons, and colored pencils. Consider the grade level of your students when selecting these materials: Larger pencils and crayons are used in the lower grades, because they are easier for the students to manipulate.

CONSIDERATIONS

- Students in grades K–2 generally use large blue pencils.
- Students in grades K–1 generally use large crayons (8 to a box).
- Students in grades 2–5 generally use thin yellow No. 2 pencils.
- Students in grades 2–5 generally use smaller crayons (12–36 to a box).
- Students in grades 2–5 use colored pencils.

Paper

Like writing and coloring utensils, paper is sized with a purpose—the more widely spaced the lines, the younger the student. Widely spaced lines are easier for younger students to use when they are learning to print, as they are just beginning to develop their fine motor skills.

CONSIDERATIONS

- Paper for kindergarten students has lines that are spaced 1⅛" apart.
- Paper for first grade students has lines that are spaced ⅝" apart.
- Paper for second and third grade students has lines that are spaced ½" apart.
- Paper for students in the fourth grade and up generally has lines that are spaced ¼" apart.
- Plain newsprint can be used for math.

Textbooks

A school district adopts textbooks in a specific series for each subject area taught. All students should receive a textbook for each subject area.

70
Textbook
Inventory

CONSIDERATIONS

- Post a number on the spine of each textbook, using a small sticker and a permanent marker.
- Assign each student a specific textbook, and keep a record of the assigned textbook number.
- Review your expectations for textbook care with the whole class.

Journals

Writing journals, which can be used by students for projects in any curricular area, are generally available at your school site.

CONSIDERATIONS

- Have students create journals for each subject area. These journals present a continuous record of what students are learning, and they are an excellent example of the students' work to show to parents at conference time.
- Make a point to summarize lessons, and model writing with the whole class.
- Create simple journals from white paper stapled inside a designated color of construction paper, with the student's name written at the top.
- Use journals in math for students to write up explanations of how particular problems were solved or to illustrate their understanding of math concepts.

Homework Folders

It is important for students to have a designated folder where they keep their homework. Home communications can be kept there as well. Students in the lower grades should have folders with covers showing their name and the specific skills they are learning (for example, colors, alphabet, numbers, shapes). Homework folders for students in the upper grades can also have illustrated covers, or perhaps be identified with just the student's name.

CONSIDERATIONS

- Require each student to have a two-pocket folder. These come in a variety of colors.
- Label the pockets "Homework" for all homework to be returned and "Paperwork" for all school notifications that need to be signed and returned.

Student Paperwork

At the beginning of the school year, there are many forms that students must have filled out and returned. Check with your school office for such paperwork, which might include emergency information cards, release of liability forms, PTA membership forms, and school behavior contracts.

CONSIDERATIONS

- Offer incentives to students for bringing necessary paperwork back.
- Keep track of what has been returned by checking off each returned sheet next to students' names on a class roster.
- Record emergency contact information in your grade book before turning information in to the office.
- Note students' allergies.

15
Class Roster

Welcome Letter

A "Welcome to My Class" letter is an excellent way to introduce yourself and spell out your policies, procedures, and expectations. Keep in mind that any correspondence that is sent home with your students needs to be approved by the school administrator before distribution. Check with fellow grade-level teachers to see if they send welcome letters home and what their letters include.

79
Welcome Letter
(sample, blank)

CONSIDERATIONS

- Keep the welcome letter short and sweet.
- Be prepared to follow through with the procedures, policies, and expectations that are spelled out in your letter.
- Include information in the welcome letter on topics such as curriculum overviews, homework policy, absentee and tardiness policies, supplies needed, resources for parents, and recommended readings.
- Translate the welcome letter into the family's home language, if possible. Check with the school office if you are unsure which language is spoken in the student's home.

Focal Point

Teacher

As a first-year teacher, you will find that being equipped with the materials you need on that first day of class will make it possible for you to focus on the students in your class. Have a place for everything, and have everything in its place. After all, being well prepared is your best strategy.

The following list of items, all of which can be kept at your desk, includes many things that can help you get off to a great start.

Referral File

Keep referrals made either to the office or to the nurse in this file.

Note File

Keep correspondence from home (such as absences and excuses) in this file.

Parental Consent File

Keep legal consent forms (such as field trip permission slips and video releases) in this file.

Referral Forms

Keep a supply of blank referral forms used by the school for times when you need to send students to the office or the nurse.

Class Roster

The class roster listing your students' names and relevant information is important for you to have well before the first day of school. It will be needed to create student name tags and desk name plates, as well as to set up your grade book or grading program. Make sure to keep a copy of this roster, or attendance sheet, as backup.

15
Class Roster

Personal Emergency Card

It is advisable to complete an emergency card with information about yourself to have on file in the office. You might include medical information, contacts, and vehicle information. Be sure to update the information as needed.

School Binder

It is helpful to have a binder specifically for school policies and procedures. Be sure to keep this binder updated with the most recent version of each document.

Your binder may contain the following items:

• School faculty roster
• Room list
• School policies and procedures, including those for inclement weather, substitutes, dismissals, shortened days, special schedules, lunch schedule, recess schedule, emergency procedures and protocol, visitors, and volunteers

Supplemental Curricular Materials

Confirm with other teachers at your grade level that you have all the necessary components for the curriculum that you are teaching. Then spend time well ahead of the first day of school to really get to know the curriculum—not only the textbook, but the supplemental materials as well. These supplemental curricular materials may be referred to as Teacher's Editions (TEs), Teacher's Manuals, or Curricular Guidebooks.

Lesson Plans

Keep up with your lesson planning! Ask your fellow teachers how and when they plan, but remember that, as a new teacher, you *must* set aside time for lesson planning, no matter what other, more experienced teachers may be doing. Make sure you protect yourself: Plan, and always have your plans available for your administrator to see. Have a full set of weekly lesson plans prepared in advance.

48, 49, 50
Lesson Plans

Focal Point

Grade Book

Maintain a grade book as a record of all assignments and assessments that are being used to measure your students' performance. Make it work for you, but always be prepared to show it to parents and/or your administrator, and have scoring rubrics on hand as well. A grade book that is complete and up-to-date shows why you are grading a student the way you are. In some schools, these records may be kept in an electronic grading program.

Supplies

Have supplies readily available to keep things running smoothly. The importance of this cannot be stressed enough. Many—if not all—supplies can be requested at your school site.

The following are important supplies to have:

- Pens—black (for legal documentation) and blue
- Pencils—sharpened No. 2 pencils
- Markers—assorted colors for posters, word cards, and headings on bulletin boards
- Permanent markers (Sharpie)—for labeling
- Overhead markers—assorted colors and transparency sheets
- Tape—Scotch, masking, bookbinding, and clear plastic
- Sticky putty—for hanging posters
- Stapler and staples
- Paper clips
- Sticky notes (Post-it Notes)
- Note paper—for correspondence with parents and other teachers
- Scissors
- Hole punch
- Lined tag board (heavy poster board)
- Sentence strips—long narrow strips for writing sentences, labels, and standards
- Word cards—shorter sentence strips for words, flash cards, and name tags
- Pointer—for instruction
- Yardstick and/or meter stick—for math measurement

First Month of Teaching

The first month of school can be a very busy one. There are many meetings to attend, procedures to establish, and policies to implement. A lot of these extra activities may require that you leave your classroom or open your classroom to visitors. The following are some suggestions that will help you stay organized and be prepared for this busy time—and for the rest of the year, too!

Back to School Night

Back to School Night is typically an open house that is held in the evening. Parents are invited to visit classrooms and meet the teachers.

CONSIDERATIONS

- Have an agenda—or guide—posted in the classroom as an orientation to the evening.
- Plan your Back to School Night to include most if not all of the following items:
  - Personal introduction—experience, hobbies
  - Textbook introductions—display textbooks either on desks or at the board in the front of the classroom
  - Daily agenda—review instructional minutes
  - Homework policy—review assignments and your grading system
  - School policies—emergency contact information, dismissal, behavior
  - Yearly calendar—review of holidays and testing dates
  - Parental support—strategies for home assistance
  - School volunteer protocol—guidelines for parents on campus
  - Attendance policies—attendance, absence, tardy, appointment

Faculty Meetings

Faculty meetings are an opportunity for administrators to update staff on changes in policy to make sure that the school is in compliance with current laws and regulations. You may be confronted with many forms, deadlines, and schedule changes.

CONSIDERATIONS

- Be on time.
- Bring a pen or pencil to use for signing in and taking notes.
- Bring a notebook to use for taking notes. It's helpful to use the same notebook for faculty meetings and for storing handouts, because you will refer to it often.
- Bring a calendar to use for entering the many meetings, appointments, and other events that are announced at faculty meetings.
- Keep agendas and important paperwork in a designated folder.

Beginning of Year Paperwork

At the start of each year, you will usually receive a checklist of paperwork that needs to be completed by yourself, by parents, and by students. Each school has a different way of organizing this, but much of the following may be expected:

- Emergency information cards for students
- Emergency procedures
- Child abuse reporting procedures
- Sexual harassment documentation
- School procedures
- School contracts
- Media release forms
- Student records
- Personal emergency contact information about yourself for the office
- Credentials
- Administrative evaluation paperwork

Emergency Procedures

If an emergency arises at your school, *you are responsible for your students and their safety.* You must be prepared for anything and (pretty much) everything.

Check the school handbook or ask in the office for information specific to your school. You can expect policies and recommendations to cover topics such as the following:

- Emergency backpack
  - Basic first aid kit
    - Band-Aids
    - Gloves
    - Antiseptic
    - Sterile gauze pads
    - Tape
  - Gum or hard candies (for long waits)
  - Comic books
  - Playing cards
  - Sunscreen
  - Water
  - Protein bars
  - Current class roster
  - Paper
  - Pencil or pen
  - Toilet paper
- Exit plan
  - Map of emergency exits
  - Exit procedures
  - Injured student protocol, including notifications
  - Items to practice with students
    - Procedures (such as drop, cover, roll)
    - Lining up (organized order, quietly)
    - Exiting—where to go? (alternate routes and strategies)
- School expectations
  - Do you have a specific role in emergencies (for example, search-and-rescue or medical)?
  - How and where do parents pick students up?

Professional Tips

Testing

Teachers today are required to take an array of examinations that demonstrate competency. Some are subject matter competency exams, while others focus on language acquisition.

The following exams may be required:

- RICA (Reading Instruction Competence Assessment)
- Single Subject Exam
- State Competency Exam
- CLAD (Certified LabVIEW Associate Developer)
- ELD (English Language Development) Exam

CONSIDERATIONS

- Extensions—Some districts allow extensions on required exams of up to five years for new teachers.
- Test preparation classes—Find out if your district has any upcoming test preparation classes. Otherwise, test preparation classes may be available through extension courses, a local community college, or online.
- Teacher publications—Check union newspapers or national teacher newspapers, as well as postings and flyers at your school site for information on competency exams.
- Explore whether taking classes at a university as either a part-time or full-time student might allow you to take exams as part of your tuition.
- Prepare for and pass tests the first time you take them. This avoids your having to re-register, pay for, and take the tests again.
- Don't put it off. Deadlines can creep up on you, and missing an examination deadline could cost you your position.

Credential Renewal

Credentials must be renewed regularly, typically every five years. Be aware of your renewal date.

CONSIDERATIONS

- Online—Many states now offer an online renewal process. Check with the Department of Education in your state about policies on teacher credentialing.
- Required hours—Evidence of professional development and continued education hours must be verified and submitted upon request. Keep documentation for the many hours you devote to professional development meetings, along with their agendas; conferences you attend; and district courses you take. Keep a file of the transcripts showing higher education classes you have completed.
- Professional development folder—Create a folder for documentation of hours spent in professional development, together with relevant agendas. If audited, you will have nothing to worry about.

Salary Point Credits

Salary point credits provide a way for teachers to move up the pay scale. For every designated number of accrued credits (also called points or units), teachers can advance a step higher on the pay scale within a specific time frame. Check with your district to see how many credits are needed for advancement.

Professional development courses are a great way to stay on top of current curriculum programs, assessment techniques, and changes in the field, all while increasing your potential to earn more money. Attending professional development courses through the district or higher education courses at a local college or university is a good way to keep current in the field, network with other teachers, and share best practices.

CONSIDERATIONS

- District-sponsored credits
  - Take advantage of the fact that credits offered by the district are usually free.
  - Remember that credits are offered for a wide range of education topics, including classroom management strategies, technology courses, cultural diversity courses, and even traveling abroad over the summer with other teachers from your district.
- University credits
  - Always verify that your district will accept university credits as salary point credits.
  - Verify unit submission procedures, guidelines, and necessary forms.
  - Keep copies of all submitted paperwork. If possible, have the date and time stamped on your copies upon submission.

Focal Point

- To find out about classes that are available to you, check flyers at school, ask other teachers, or look through union and teacher periodicals.
- Some courses are held in satellite locations; others are offered after school or on Saturdays.
- Online courses and programs may be available.
- In hands-on courses, much of the actual work is done on-site. These courses typically focus on practical lessons and activities across the curriculum.

Sharing Personal Information

It's a great idea, as a new teacher, to share information about yourself with others—but be selective. Be mindful of how much you share, and with whom. It's up to you to decide what you share about your professional life with your peers. In terms of what you share about your personal life, however, keep things close until you get to know everyone else better. Information you share about yourself with adult faculty members will also be very different from what you decide to share with your students.

CONSIDERATIONS

- **Personal stories**—Sharing personal stories with students is a fantastic way to develop interpersonal relationships and gain students' trust.
  - Be mindful of what you share.
  - Always think from the perspective of the parents. What stories would be okay for their child to hear?
  - Shared stories could include the following:
    - Your travels
    - Your own education experiences
    - Your interests in movies, music, musical instruments, athletics
- **E-mail address**—E-mail is sometimes the easiest way for parents to keep in touch with you.
  - Be prepared to receive and respond to all correspondences.
  - Do not give out your personal e-mail address.
  - Give out only your professional e-mail address, if you choose to correspond with parents through e-mail.
  - Remember that professional e-mail can serve as documentation.

- **Phone number**—It is not recommended to give students or their parents your personal phone number, though this is a personal choice.
  - Receiving calls—Provide the school's phone number. Parents can call and leave you a message.
  - Making calls—Use the school phone to avoid having your personal phone number show up on caller ID.
- **Discussions**—Keep discussions at work on a professional level, even if you are comfortable with your colleagues.
  - Does what you are discussing relate to school?
  - Is what you are sharing confidential student information?
  - Would you say this to an administrator or parent?
  - Is the conversation merely school gossip or hearsay? Don't get caught up in it.
- **Photographs**—Bring personal pictures into class as a way to share your life with students.
  - Share only pictures that are school-appropriate and relevant to class discussion.
  - Remember that a picture is worth a thousand words—be careful what you share.

Keeping Students Engaged at the Front of the Classroom

There are a variety of teaching tools that can be used to deliver instruction. Utilizing them correctly will maximize their potential as they assist you and your students in your presentations. Your choice of teaching tools will depend on the options available at your school site, but it should further reflect your own preferences.

The Board

Whether you use a chalkboard or a whiteboard, it is at the board where most of the direct instruction takes place in the classroom.

CONSIDERATIONS

- Keep the board easily accessible.
- Make the board the focal point of the room. All students should be able to see it easily.
- Post your name, the date, the daily agenda, key standards to be covered, and the student count (boys, girls, total) every day.
- Tips and tricks to help you maximize the benefit of the board in your classroom include the following:
  - Flat paintbrushes work well for cleaning chalk trays, allowing you to sweep the chalk dust directly into a dustpan.
  - Old socks make great erasers for whiteboards.
  - You can remove permanent marker from a whiteboard by tracing over the marks with a dry-erase marker and then erasing it.
  - Some boards are magnetic, which makes them a handy place for temporarily posting student work, instructional charts, or posters. Keep the magnets in one corner for easy access.

Screens

Screens are needed for projection when using an ELMO projector, LCD projector, document reader, or overhead projector. Screens are permanently installed in many classrooms.

CONSIDERATIONS

- Use a whiteboard to project onto, if one is available.
- Project onto butcher paper if no screen or whiteboard is available.
- Test the setup before using it, adjusting the distance and focus of the equipment.

Maps

Geography is very important, but it is often lacking in the daily curriculum. Using maps can be a fun and interactive way for students to learn geography.

CONSIDERATIONS

- Check the maps that are available in your classroom. Are they relevant to the curriculum?
- Make good use of the state, continent, and world maps that are often attached to the top of the chalkboard, whiteboard, or bulletin board for easy access.
- Practice using maps, and have the students interact with them as well.
- Know your map terminology: legend or key, scale, compass rose, longitude, and latitude.
- Choose a location and challenge students to find it. "Where is Fiji?" Make this a daily challenge. Students can also research the location, for example, "What industries are in Fiji?" "What do Fijians eat?" "What language do they speak in Fiji?"

Overhead Projector

Overhead projectors have always been popular teaching tools. They allow the teacher to present and model written material to the whole class at the same time.

CONSIDERATIONS

- Keep the projector in an accessible location so that it is easy to set up.
- Keep the owner's manual and refer to it when needed.
- Take care with the cord placement. Tripping over the cord could cause an accident, resulting in injury and/or damage to the projector.
- Look for overhead instructional sets, especially for math (for example, money sets, shape sets, fractions). Keep these sets in a storage container near the overhead projector for easy access.

- Keep working "overhead pens" in a variety of colors near the projector.
- Make sure you have a working bulb and an extra bulb for backup.
- Use overhead transparency sheets. These can be held under running water and rinsed clean.
- Make copies on overhead transparency sheets to model work for students. These can be stored in plastic sleeves, which can be written on with overhead markers. Rinse the sleeves clean and store them in a binder for future use.
- Use overhead transparencies with small groups of students so that they can record their work on them and then present it to the class.
- Keep a roll of paper towels and a spray bottle of water handy for cleaning the projector.

ELMO Projector or Document Reader

An ELMO projector or document reader can transmit images directly from a document hard copy, a computer screen, or even what is on a teacher's desk to a large screen for viewing by the entire class. This type of equipment is a valuable teaching tool, because it allows students to see actual demonstrations of lessons. More and more, it is replacing the overhead projector in the classroom.

CONSIDERATIONS

- Set up the equipment and practice with it before using it with the children.
- Take care with the cord placement. Tripping over the cord could cause an accident, resulting in injury and/or damage to the equipment.
- If a bulb "dies," turn off the equipment, let it rest for a few minutes, and then try again. A bulb may fail temporarily but not yet be burned out. Bulbs can be expensive, and it's worth it to try to avoid unnecessary replacement.
- When not in use, the equipment should be turned off to conserve the bulb's life.
- Always store the equipment in a secure place.

LCD Projector

An LCD projector allows teachers to display many types of media, including pictures, images, student-made videos, PowerPoint presentations, and lecture notes—all of which can be stored on a laptop computer. You can even type in students' oral contributions during discussions for immediate display.

- Set up the projector and practice with it before using it with the children.
- Establish a connection between the laptop and the projector, typically by pressing the F5 key and the command key simultaneously.
- Use an adapter that comes with a Mac laptop in order to connect the laptop to the LCD projector.
- Use the projector for computer instruction of programs like Microsoft Word. If students are sitting at individual computers, they can follow the lesson and practice each step as it is modeled on the LCD projector.

Teacher Tools Station

Establishing a teacher tools station with everything you need right at your fingertips is important for smooth delivery of instruction. This can be a drawer storage bin on wheels positioned next to either the teacher's seat or the presentation equipment (such as an overhead projector or ELMO projector). It could also be a designated drawer of your desk if you do most of your presenting at your desk.

CONSIDERATIONS

- Practice your planned daily routine: Think to yourself, "What do I need to present this lesson?" Stock your teacher tools station accordingly.
- Suggested tools for your teacher tools station include the following:
  - Stapler, staples, masking tape, Scotch tape, paper clips, and scissors
  - Tissues, paper towels, lined and plain paper, Post-it Notes, notepaper, pens, pencils, erasers, and markers
  - Word cards, math flash cards, and extra blank word cards
  - Dry-erase markers and cleaning spray if using a whiteboard
  - Stickers, rewards, and incentives that you are using (tickets, coupons, tokens)

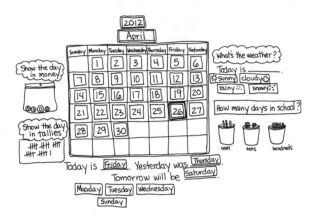

The Calendar as a Teaching Tool

A calendar provides a wealth of instruction opportunities across many grade levels. Lower grades (K through grade 2) use the calendar as part of a daily morning routine. Upper grades (Grades 3 through 6) might use the calendar primarily for math.

CONSIDERATIONS

- Use calendars that are either store-bought or created from poster board.
- Consider having students create the numbers—for example, by illustrating numbered squares that you prepare for them. The squares can be related by theme to a specific unit or holiday season.
- Consider relating the numbers by shape to the months they represent—for example, pumpkins for October or turkeys for November. Pattern recognition can be taught by alternating shapes.
- Consider including bilingual labels for the months and days of the calendar for English Language Development (ELD) support.
- Appoint a calendar monitor to lead the class in calendar activities. This gives you time to get ready for the day, and it empowers the students.

Grades K–2

CONSIDERATIONS

- Review the days of the week and the number of days in a month: "What day is the fourth day of this month?" "What day is the second Tuesday of this month?" "How many Wednesdays are in this month?"
- Review the weather: "Today is _____ (sunny, cloudy, foggy, rainy, snowy, hot, cold, mild, etc.)." All of these weather terms can be written on cards and illustrated for ELD support.
- Review "Today is _____," "Yesterday was _____," "Tomorrow will be _____."
- Review counting by twos, threes, fours, etc.
- Create and review patterns with numbers and colors (for example, red-red-blue).
- Create "ones" and "tens" groups using items such as coffee stirrers or popsicle sticks. Start with one, then two, then three, etc. Once you have ten, they can be bundled and placed in a "tens" container. This can be done monthly, and after a time the class will bundle a "hundreds" group.
- Represent the date with money, counting out coins to symbolize the date. The 12th of the month could be represented by one dime and two pennies, two nickels and two pennies, or twelve pennies.
- Represent each day that passes with tally marks.

Grades 3–6

CONSIDERATIONS

- Assign research projects related to the history of the date—for example, each student is assigned a date to research for that month and reports out on that day.
- Assign math problems that equal the date—for example, on the 14th of the month you could assign $(3 + 4) \times 4 \div 2 = 14$, or if $b - 6 = 8$, then $b = 14$.
- Work with students to calculate the day on which a date would fall next year, in three years, etc.
- Work with students to calculate the percentage and fractional part of the total number of days in the month for any given date—for example, for the 4th of the month you could calculate $4 \div 30 = 2 \div 15$ of the month, .1333 of the month, and 13% of the month.
- Use conversions to illustrate the date—for example, for the 3rd of the month you might use 3 feet = 36 inches, 3°C = 37°F, or 3 pints = ⅜ gallons.
- Having students write a poem or journal entry using the same number of sentences as the number of the date—for example, for the 4th of the month, students would write four sentences for the assignment.

The Common Area

In most classrooms for kindergarten through grade 3, teachers set up a common area (often a rug, which provides a well-defined space) where students meet to cover lessons and share out. In classrooms for grades 4 through 6, while there may or may not be a designated rug area, there is often a space in the front or "north" part of the room for the same types of activities. In both grade levels, a designated common area as part of your classroom design is important.

Whole Class Instruction

The teacher presents lessons to the whole class as a collective group. This is the most common way to present a lesson, and it is an excellent way to monitor students' attention and understanding.

Think-Pair-Share

Students share responses with one another for teacher-prompted questions or thoughts.

CONSIDERATIONS
- Give enough time for every student to share.
- Rotate pairs with each question.
- Have pairs share with other pairs for further discussion.

Listening to Stories

Students gather to listen while the teacher reads stories aloud from picture books or chapter books.

CONSIDERATIONS

- Reading to students is essential to improving their comprehension when they read for themselves.
- Reading motivates students to read on their own.
- Older students, as well as younger students, enjoy being read to.
- Students can write summaries, change endings, write letters to characters, or write reviews after listening to a story.
- Consider reading short stories or poems.
- Following are our top suggestions for multicultural authors and series:
  - Alma Flor Ada (Latino stories)
  - Arnold Adoff (African American stories)
  - Eric Carle (science-related stories)
  - Chicken Soup series
  - Sandra Cisneros (Latino families)
  - Tomie dePaola (Native American stories)
  - Mem Fox (rhythm and rhyme books)
  - Carmen Lomas Garza (Latino families)
  - Paul Goble (Native American stories)
  - Virginia Hamilton (African American stories)
  - Francisco Jiménez (Latino stories)
  - Gerald McDermott (trickster tales)
  - Naomi Shihab Nye (Middle Eastern literature)
  - Patricia Polacco (family stories)
  - Jack Prelutsky (poetry)
  - Dr. Seuss (rhythm and rhyme books)
  - Shel Silverstein (poetry)
  - Gary Soto (Latino stories)
  - John Steptoe (African American stories)

Small Group Work

30
Group Organizer

31
Group Rotation Planner

In small group instruction, you can review skills with students or introduce level-appropriate activities to groups.

CONSIDERATIONS

- Use teacher-directed activities, with either one group or several groups, to utilize the space.
- Assign groups of mixed levels so that all students can be supported.
- Consider assigning roles to group members (such as reporter, recorder, illustrator, clarifier) to make sure that all students participate.

Presentations

Students gather in the common area or face the focal point to listen to their classmates share their work or present their findings to the class on a given project or topic.

CONSIDERATIONS

- Have a special chair—an Author's Chair—for students to sit in while sharing their stories, projects, or presentations.
- Use a podium or designated desk for students in the upper grades.
- Set up a desk with a projector for use in presenting, if the equipment is available and appropriate for the presentation.

Demonstrations

Use the common area or focal point of the room for demonstrating procedures and experiments.

CONSIDERATIONS

- Be prepared.
- Practice procedures or experiments before presenting them to students.

Conflict Resolution

Discuss issues and problems between students in a constructive way for the whole class. These issues or problems may have arisen either inside or outside the classroom.

21
Conflict
Resolution Slip

CONSIDERATIONS

- Establish a time limit and consider using a timer to limit student talk time, perhaps 5 to 10 minutes.
- Set rules for discussion, for example, "One student speaks at a time" and "Students hear both sides prior to making any decisions."

Homework Review

Recap homework assignments and/or the day's activities for the whole class.

CONSIDERATIONS

- Explain and model the homework for that night.
- Offer clarification where needed.
- Review what was learned and write it on the board. This can serve as the next day's morning journal entry.
- Use this focused 5 to 10 minutes at the end of the day to help the students settle down, since the end of the day can be a bit chaotic.

Bulletins and School News

Designate a specific bulletin board near the front of the room for posting bulletins and flyers with information on school activities. Proximity to the classroom door makes it easily accessible to parents and visitors.

CONSIDERATIONS

- Create a catchphrase for your board, for example, "Extra, Extra" or "Read All About It!"
- Keep the board updated with current information, and remove outdated information promptly.
- Read all new information to students prior to posting it; post and refer to it daily.

Daily and Weekly Homework Posting

A handout for the week's assigned homework keeps students in the know and helps you stay on schedule.

73, 74
Weekly
Homework

CONSIDERATIONS

- Provide students with clear and detailed expectations.
- Include any or all of the following in the homework posting:
  - Assignments and expectations
  - Weekly spelling words and a daily activity for words each night, Monday through Thursday. An activity could be alphabetizing, writing sentences, creating a story, illustrating, or defining.
  - Daily minutes of reading, possibly including a list of relevant book titles or topics
  - Relevant websites
  - Extra credit
  - Extension assignments
  - Extra practice
  - Challenge

School or District Bulletin

School or district bulletins may include school and district news items, a calendar, or both.

CONSIDERATIONS

- Review the bulletin and/or calendar with your students before posting it.
- School or district bulletins often include a schedule of upcoming events, happenings, and announcements.
- School or district bulletins are typically sent home weekly or monthly.

Parent Newsletter

A parent newsletter keeps everyone informed, and it's an excellent way to share classroom news with the students' families.

53
Newsletter
(sample, blank)

CONSIDERATIONS

- Decide if you will send a newsletter weekly, biweekly, or monthly. Be sure to send it out on a regular schedule throughout the school year.
- Include items such as classroom happenings, writing samples, art, announcements, suggested websites, suggested reading titles related to current units of study, acknowledgements to volunteers, and items needed from a classroom wish list.
- Read the newsletter with students before sending it home with them.
- Save your newsletters to use as a template for the next school year.

Reminders and Handouts

A wide variety of other information is provided to students and their families on an almost daily basis. Reminders may be for picture day, PTA meeting dates, upcoming fundraisers, and special events like performances or curriculum nights. Handouts include everything from community flyers to district-approved programs and school letters.

CONSIDERATIONS

- Share all handouts with students before sending them home.
- Remove items from the board once they are outdated.

Field Trip Information

Details about field trips and reminders about field trip day will be accessible to both students and parents if posted on this designated bulletin board.

CONSIDERATIONS

- Items to be posted include extra permission slips, due dates for money, and a sign-up sheet for parent volunteers interested in helping.
- Post field trip items as early as possible, and remove them when the date has passed.

Attention-Getters
and What They Mean

It is essential to have an attention-getter—or signal—that gets the attention of your students quickly and effectively. Not only does it demonstrate a command of your class and make for smooth transitions between activities, but it is also extremely important in the case of an emergency.

Keep your attention-getter simple, quick, and safe. Make sure that it isn't disruptive to other classrooms. Teachers use a variety of attention-getters. Choose one or more that you feel comfortable with.

USES

- Transitioning from one subject to the next
- Closing a topic or period
- Preparing for clean-up
- Moving to the next activity
- Focusing on the teacher for directions
- Quieting students for announcements or directions

CONSIDERATIONS

- Be consistent.
- Practice.
- Be calm and in control: Use a signal once and wait. Never try the signal over and over, because students will not take it seriously.
- Move closer to a student who is not responding to the signal. Proximity can make a big difference in the response you get.
- Remember that you are in charge, and hold your ground when students test you. A strong, silent teacher holding his or her ground can be very intimidating.
- Consider having students help decide on a signal.
- Ask students to list classroom signals that have been used in their other classes.
- Find several classroom signals that work for you, and alternate them if one becomes less effective.

Holding Two Fingers Up in a "Peace Sign"

Nothing is said out loud; two fingers are held up in a V shape, or peace sign. Each student is to hold a hand up as soon as they see this signal, which cues other students who have not yet seen the teacher's signal. "When hands are up, mouths are shut, and eyes are on teacher." This is very effective when your class is around other classes: You remain calm and collected, not saying a word, and just wait for all of your students to respond.

USES

- Refocusing students' attention from group work
- Assembling in the common area
- Quieting students down when entering the classroom

Whistle

This signal is only used outside. It is a quick but loud way to grab students' attention.

USES

- Calling students inside when they are outside the building
- Transitioning to another activity when outdoors

Egg Timer, Bell, and Stopwatch

The egg timer, bell, and stopwatch all provide an excellent way to pace your instruction. The bell or ring tone should signal the completion of an activity and a transition to what follows: Stop, straighten up, wait for directions, and/or transition to the next activity.

USES

- Rotating small groups through a series of activities
- Timing assessments
- Transitioning between subjects
- Timing discussions and presentations

Patterned Clap

The teacher claps a pattern, and the students then repeat the patterned clap to show that they are ready. Students can also help create patterns to be used for a certain period of time. Always practice the patterns so that the response becomes automatic.

USES

- Quieting the class during a busy activity or when it is time to focus
- Refocusing the class after sharing out in groups

Focal Point

Maracas, Tambourines, and Hand Drums

Instruments can be a fun way to call for students' attention.

USES

- Transitioning to a different activity
- Quieting and calming students
- Signaling clean-up time
- Signaling preparation for going home
- Signaling a specific activity

CONSIDERATIONS

- Designate students to be signal monitors, cued by the teacher.
- Use different instruments for different subjects or different times of the day.
- Use this tactic if you have one or two difficult students who need an opportunity to be in charge of something. You'll be surprised at how engaged and on task such students can be when they are given a responsibility such as this.

Turn Lights Off

Turn the lights off, pause, then turn them back on. This is an immediate attention-getter, a signal usually used when all else fails. Reserve this signal for use as the "Ultimate Attention-Getter."

USES

- Getting attention instantly in a busy classroom
- Signaling clean-up time at the end of the day

Hands on Your Head

The teacher places both hands on his or her head, and the students follow suit. This assures that all activity stops and that attention is on the speaker. This is a common signal for students in kindergarten and grade 1.

USES

- Intercom announcements
- Signaling an emergency

Countdown

The teacher holds five fingers in the air and counts down silently (or quietly) toward zero: 5 = stop, 4 = tell your neighbor to stop, 3 = look at the teacher, 2 = listen, 1 = wait for a cue to begin the next activity. (Another version of this signal is called "give me five," where the teacher counts up: 1 = stop, 2 = tell your neighbor to stop, 3 = look at the teacher, 4 = listen, 5 = wait for a cue to begin the next activity.)

USES

- Signaling transitions
- Silently signaling during assemblies
- Signaling on fieldtrips

Navigating the Curriculum with Teacher's Editions, Curriculum Guides, and Standards

You have been given Teacher's Editions (TEs) for each of the subject areas that you teach. Each of these Teacher's Editions may also come with other supplemental resources, including but not limited to student consumable workbooks, transparencies, CDs and DVDs, worksheet masters, manipulatives, and assessment masters. While all of these items are relevant to the subject being taught, where do you start? What should you focus on first? Is there a pacing guide? Should you go from the beginning of the textbook to the end, or can you skip around based on your students' needs?

CONSIDERATIONS

- Start off with the basics.
- Don't get overwhelmed.
- Refer to the inventory breakdown found in the front of the Teacher's Editions to confirm that you have what you need.
- Consult fellow grade-level teachers for insights, overviews, and advice.
- The Teacher's Edition is a rich resource that offers valuable help for working with a specific textbook.
  - Use the TE to walk yourself through an actual lesson, examining all of the student resources and components.
  - Review the objectives and standards that are relevant to the lessons.

- Additional support is available to you within your school or district.
  - School or district curriculum coordinator
  - Vice-Principal and/or Principal
  - Veteran or mentor teacher at your grade level
  - Professional development and training opportunities
    - Help you understand how to navigate through the curriculum
    - Assist you with content standards for your grade level
- Online support is available from the textbook publisher as well as third-party educational websites.
  - Support with the materials from the publisher's website
  - Lesson plans and shortcuts from teacher websites
- Veteran teachers are an excellent source of guidance.
  - Veteran teachers have the experience to help new teachers in many areas, including the following:
    - Understanding your situation, because they've been in your shoes
    - Advice based on their having experienced a series of different curriculum changes during their tenure
    - What to focus on and how to include supplemental materials
    - Knowing how to meet the needs of different student learning styles
    - Offering a variety of strategies and best practices
  - Request a recommendation from your principal if you aren't sure whom to ask for help.
  - Imitate a veteran teacher's approach when you sense that it will work for you. In time, you will become more creative, and you will make the curriculum yours.
- State content standards are listed on the Department of Education website for each state.
  - The state's Department of Education website lists the subject area standards that are expected to be introduced at each grade level.
  - The state's website will help you in your planning from the Teacher's Edition.
  - Many of the textbook series adopted by the state will list or refer to the state content standards in each lesson.
- Always ask for help.
  - When in doubt, ask.
  - Remember that good teachers are always open to new ideas.
  - Keep learning, and keep trying new things.
  - Don't forget that grade-level team members are teaching the same material, and they may have great advice.
  - Surround yourself with positive teachers who are excited about what they do.

Working with Parents

02
Aide/Volunteer
To-Do List

Working with parents can make your job easier. Parental support—from volunteering in your classroom to assisting the child at home—can be invaluable.

CONSIDERATIONS

- Parental support in the classroom can take many forms, all under your guidance.
  - **Manage** their help with explicit instructions and clear expectations.
  - **Set boundaries**, and always maintain your professionalism.
  - **Acknowledge** parents: Take time to say "hello" every time they come into the classroom.
  - **Reach out** to parents, perhaps inviting them to school once a month or once a semester for coffee and donuts before school. This offers them an opportunity to visit before the school day begins, which for many parents is the best time to meet.

53
Newsletter
(sample, blank)

71, 72
Weekly
Assessment

- Parental support at home can be facilitated, so that the child benefits to the greatest extent possible.
  - **Encourage partnership.** When parents act as partners in the child's education, they are an integral part of their child's academic success.
  - **Stay positive.** Make an initial call home to share something positive. It is better for the first call to be positive rather than negative.
  - **Communicate** with parents regularly. Whether it is through a weekly newsletter or simply having them sign tests or quizzes, it is important to keep parents updated.
  - **Avoid surprises** by notifying parents if their child may not be passing. Schools usually have a form that needs to be sent home before report cards are issued.

- Teacher-parent-student meetings are an opportunity to explore how the teacher, student, and parent can work together to the advantage of the student's education.

18
Conference
Calendar
19
Conference
Reminder
20
Conference
Sign-Up Letter

  - **Establish a sense of collaboration** by positioning yourself beside the parents, rather than in front of them, because the side-by-side position will be perceived as less adversarial.
  - **Listen** to both the parent and the student, and avoid dominating the conversation.
  - **Don't take it personally** when a parent disagrees with you or offers advice. Say, "Thank you for your perspective, I hadn't though of it that way before. I will consider your advice."
  - **Be clear and consistent.** Explain what you, as the teacher, expect in terms of behavior, your discipline plan, homework expectations, and attendance expectations.
  - **Stay positive.** Use language that is positive, even when stating a negative.

56
Report Card /
Cumulative
Record
Comments

Focal Point

The Door:
Entry and Exit Procedures

32
Hall Passes

The classroom door offers dual access—into your classroom world and out to the outside world. How you handle entry and exit through this door is very important. Having well-defined procedures is critical to the safety and well-being of your students, as well as to adhering to district policy.

CONSIDERATIONS

- **Volunteers**
  - Schools have policies that cover volunteers who work in the classroom, which may include the following:
    - Checking in at the office upon entering and exiting the school
    - Obtaining a pass or badge
    - Proof of a negative tuberculosis (TB) test
    - Completing specific training
  - Prepare a designated work area with a specific schedule or specific activities for them to support.
- **Student volunteers**—Students from a higher grade often like to volunteer in a classroom for a lower grade.
  - Arrange with other teachers for a student volunteer.
  - Confirm times and schedule with the student and his or her classroom teacher.
  - Prepare a schedule and activities for the student volunteer to follow.
  - Provide the student volunteer with a hall pass to carry when en route to and from your classroom.

- **Visitors**—On certain occasions, you may have a parent visitor or guest in your classroom.
  - Get permission from your administrator for visitors.
  - Have visitors sign in and sign out.
  - Have visitors pick up a visitor pass or badge from the office if school policy requires it.
- **Students picked up early**—Parents may pick students up for appointments or other necessary activities.
  - Have the designated parent or guardian sign the student out.
  - Obtain the official release form before the student is released from your classroom.
  - Save all release forms for your records.
- **Students exiting and returning to the classroom**—There are times when a student needs to leave the classroom, for example, to use the restroom, pick up something from the office, or retrieve something from the play area.
  - Always send students in pairs (to reduce your liability).
  - Provide students with a hall pass.
  - Establish a firm exiting policy, which may include the following:
    - Students must raise their hand to ask permission.
    - Exiting is never permitted during direct instruction time.
    - Students must carry a hall pass.
- **Students exiting classroom**—A student sometimes needs to leave the classroom but returning is not immediate (for example, going to the nurse, seeing an administrator, or testing).
  - Send two students with the exiting student. Once the exiting student has been dropped off, the two students can return together.
  - Provide students with a hall pass.
  - Send any necessary referral paperwork with the student.
- **Whole class exiting classroom**—It is important to establish an efficient exit policy and to train the students in it. This is critical when exiting in an emergency.
  - Non-emergency exit
    - Use a system such as excusing students by tables, excusing all students wearing pants, excusing those students who have a birthday in January, then in February, and so on.
    - Make non-emergency exits from the classroom into a game: Pull a student's name from a deck of cards or popsicle sticks, then ask them a question, such as a math problem or the capital of a state. As students answer correctly, they get to line up.
    - Require students with behavior problems during exiting to return to their seats and wait to exit until all the other students have been called.

- Emergency exit
  - Follow a specific exiting order, such as desk 1, desk 2, and so on.
  - Establish specific procedures and rules, for example, "no talking" and "push in chairs."
  - Remember that practice makes perfect.
  - Maintain quiet lines.
  - Proceed to the designated area.
- **Classroom door policy**
  - A closed door could indicate "Do not disturb" before the school day begins, at recess, at lunch, or during the teacher's preparation or break times.
  - An open door could indicate that students can enter with permission.
  - **Never be alone with a student**. Whenever you are in the classroom with a student, make sure that there are at least two students in the classroom and that a door is open. Make it a practice to stand in the hall while a student retrieves a forgotten item.
- **Leaving school for field trips**—When leaving the school for a field trip, establish a timeline, which might include any or all of the following:

24
Field Trip
Checklist

25
Field Trip
Roster

  - Submit all necessary paperwork and secure transportation.
  - Invite parent volunteers. Plan for one adult for every 5 to 10 students.
  - Submit a request for school lunches.
  - Acquire or put together a first aid kit.
  - Have appropriate permission slips signed. Leave the school's portion in the office, and carry the portion with student contact information with you.
  - Include the school name and phone number on student identification tags, but avoid including the students' names, which could be called out by a stranger.
- **Whole class leaving the classroom but staying on the school campus**— Sometimes you and your class leave the classroom but remain on campus. It is important to let others know where you are.

14
Classroom
Door Sign

  - Post a sign outside your door. Include your destination, which might include the following: We're _____.
    - in Room _____
    - in Art Class
    - in the Auditorium
    - in the Assembly Room
    - in the Computer Lab
    - on a Field Trip
    - in the Garden
    - in the Gymnasium
    - in the Library
    - in the Lunch Room
    - in the Music Room
    - at P.E.
    - at Recess
  - Include the specific time period when you will be out of the classroom.
  - Ask a student monitor to be in charge of the sign.

SOUTH

Teacher's Space

On the South side of the classroom you're likely to find the teacher's desk and computer. This is where professional tasks and record keeping take place.

In this section, we provide reminders, overviews, and tools that will assist you in meeting professional obligations and managing record keeping. Included are several practical ideas and pages of advice about fitting into your new school, taking charge of your professional experience, becoming familiar with some of the most important situations new teachers often face, and where to turn for assistance.

Look for help with the following:

Who to Know and Where to Go on Campus

Many people play an integral part in keeping a school campus running, and you'll want to get to know them. These people support your job in and out of the classroom.

CONSIDERATIONS

- Take time to greet everyone, even if just with a smile and a quick "hello."
- Write down names and jobs of staff members as you meet them.
- When you need something, ask—don't tell. Your tone is important.

62
School
Personnel
Roster

The Principal

It is important for you to know your principal well.

CONSIDERATIONS

- Realize that your administrator sets the tone of the school—it is "his" or "her" school.
- Remember that administrators are a great resource—from assistance with parents and students to help with the curriculum and school or district policy.
- Establish a relationship with your administrator by checking in now and then to share information about how you are doing.

Teacher's Space

The Vice-Principal

The vice-principal, or assistant administrator, is second in command, although not all schools have one.

CONSIDERATIONS

- Recognize that an assistant administrator often wears many hats.
- The vice-principal is often the "go to" person for many issues, including the following:
  - Student referrals
  - Behavior issues
  - Meeting individual student goals
  - Planning for conferences and/or meetings with parents

Office Manager

The office manager facilitates the running of the school.

CONSIDERATIONS

- Build a good relationship with the office manager; this person can be of great assistance.
- Office managers have varied responsibilities, but most people in this position have responsibilities that include the following:
  - Classroom keys
  - Payroll
  - Ordering supplies
  - Arranging for a substitute

Plant Manager

The plant manager oversees the building and grounds maintenance and operations—a job that is physically demanding and never-ending.

CONSIDERATIONS

- Take time to say "hello" and build a relationship with the plant manager.
- The plant manager can assist you with many key school-related tasks, including the following:
  - Campus access
  - Classroom clean-ups
  - Equipment maintenance
  - Special school events

Custodial Staff

School custodians keep the school and your classroom operational and clean so that you can do your job.

CONSIDERATIONS

- Don't take custodians for granted.
- Treat custodians with respect.
- Coordinate with the custodial staff to make their job easier. Ask them questions such as "When can I put the chairs up for sweeping?" and "Where can I leave my trashcans to make it easier to empty them?"
- Find out the school's expectations for them and for you with regard to cleaning your classroom—for example, do they sweep or do you?

Resource Personnel

Resource personnel offer special services to students; they may work from a designated classroom or office.

CONSIDERATIONS

- Coordinate with resource personnel as they work with students to support Individualized Education Plan (IEP) and 504 Plan goals.
- Know the resource personnel in your school or district, and work with them to support your students' needs. This is essential to addressing the needs of your students.
- Other resource positions might include the following:
  - Drop-out prevention specialist
  - Reading specialist
  - Speech and language specialist
  - Curriculum specialist
  - Coach (reading, writing, math, etc.)
  - Nurse
  - Psychologist
  - Counselor
  - Computer lab coordinator
  - Special program coordinator
  - Grant coordinator

Advice and Recommendations for Success

Although your first teaching assignment may be overwhelming at times, it is crucial to take care of yourself along the way. The better you are, the better your teaching and classroom management will be.

CONSIDERATIONS

- Don't panic! First-day jitters are common.
  - Keep a balance in your personal life.
  - Exercise.
  - Go dancing.
  - Listen to music.
  - Read.
  - Travel.
  - Draw.
  - Go to the movies.
- Keep a clear mind. Be focused and ready to educate.
  - Be aware of student engagement and behavior.
  - Be consistent and follow through.
  - Be confident. You can do this!
  - Be open to learning from your mistakes and trying new things.
  - Be prepared.
  - Be well rested. Get plenty of sleep.
  - Be a good listener.
  - Be professional.

- Take care of yourself.
  - Carry a bottle of water.
  - Keep protein bars or an emergency snack on hand.
  - Wear comfortable shoes.
  - Keep a jacket or sweater handy.
- Stay balanced and strong.
  - Keep moving. Don't get in the habit of just sitting—move around!
  - To keep things fresh, try new approaches, ideas, and lessons.
  - Attend professional developments, trainings, and in-services.
  - Visit other classrooms.

54
Professional
Development
Log

Do's and Don'ts

School policies, legalities, and ethical responsibilities lend themselves to a host of "do's" and "don'ts." These will vary by school, district, and state. It is important to know what is expected of you.

CONSIDERATIONS

- Check the following resources for policies and responsibilities at your school:
  - School administrators
  - Resource personnel
  - Office staff
  - Mentor teacher
  - Fellow teachers
  - School or district handbook
  - District-sponsored workshops and professional developments
- Ask before you act. If in doubt, ask to make sure you have clearance.
- Don't get too comfortable. Stand by the school and/or district policy and protocols.
- Don't assume anything. The fact that another teacher is doing something outside the school's policies and protocols doesn't give you permission to do the same thing.

Do's

- Familiarize yourself with the school bell schedule.
  - Know what the first morning bell means.
  - Know when the school day officially starts.
  - Know the recess schedule for your grade level.
  - Know the lunch schedule for your grade level.
  - Know end-of-day times and procedures.
  - Know what the various bell signals mean (for example, "code red," "lockdown," "principal needs to call the office").

- Know the school staff, including job descriptions (who does what), availability, and their base of operations.
  - Administrator
  - Assistant administrator
  - Office staff
  - Grade-level lead teachers
  - Resource teachers
  - Speech and language teachers
  - School nurse
  - Counselor
  - Psychologist
  - Librarian
  - Computer lab coordinator
  - Curriculum coordinator
  - Union representative
  - Plant manager
  - Custodial staff
  - Cafeteria staff

62
School
Personnel
Roster

- Know the school and district policy on reporting child abuse.
  - What is considered child abuse?
  - When do I report child abuse?
  - To whom do I report?
  - What paperwork is necessary to properly report child abuse?
- Know how to arrange for a substitute teacher.
  - How do I request a substitute? What is the phone number to use for requesting one?
  - How do I prepare for a substitute?
  - Is there a school-recommended list of substitute teachers?

67
Substitute
Teacher
Checklist
69
Substitute
Teacher
Information

- Know your grade-level chairs, representatives, and lead teachers.
  - Teachers in these roles understand grade-level standards.
  - These teachers are especially familiar with school policy, paperwork, and deadlines.
- Understand your contract and know what is expected of you as a certificated employee with your district.
  - Know your rights.
  - Know how to request a day off and arrange for a substitute teacher.
  - Know what constitutes sexual harassment.
  - Know the procedures for the formal evaluation process.
  - Know your required contract hours for the school day.
  - Know the mandated professional development schedule and requirements for curriculum training.
  - Know if you are required to register for any new or beginning teacher training programs.

Teacher's Space

Don'ts

- Never give out your home phone number or home e-mail address. Instead, consider one or more of the following as a way of communicating with parents:
  - Give parents the school phone number and your professional e-mail address.
  - Design a teacher website so that parents can contact you through the website.
  - Send home a weekly progress report, and be sure to encourage parents to write back with any questions or concerns.
- Don't speak up in meetings unless you are clear about what is being discussed or requested. Instead, be prepared and thoughtful when you do speak up.
  - Know exactly what the discussion is about before coming into a meeting with complaints.
  - Formulate your responses in a productive manner and offer potential solutions.
  - Recruit your mentor to speak on your behalf until you feel confident doing so yourself.
- Don't get out of the habit of creating well-detailed lesson plans, because lesson plans are as important for you as they are for your students.
  - Stay in the habit of preparing complete and detailed lessons, since you will be formally evaluated several times during your first couple of years.
  - Realize that, as a new teacher, you must be more disciplined about lesson planning than more experienced teachers may need to be.
- Don't forget to dress appropriately, and remember that you are a role model for your students.
  - Be professional—and that includes how you dress.
  - Respond to administrators and colleagues respectfully.
  - Be thoughtful about how you organize conversations with parents.

71, 72
Weekly
Assessments

48, 49, 50
Lesson Plans

29
Formal
Evaluation
Checklist

- Don't stop taking care of your own health. Instead, remember that you must take good care of yourself in order to be able to take care of others.
  - Continue exercising, eating healthy foods, and getting enough sleep.
  - Be well prepared and aware of all requirements.
  - Remember: What you don't get done today, you can finish tomorrow.
- Don't let your guard down. Remember that you are responsible for many aspects of your students' lives in your position as teacher.
  - Never touch any children in a questionable way.
  - Never give rides to students.
  - Never swear in front of students, colleagues, other school personnel, or parents.
  - Never serve foods that contain known allergens.
  - Never be alone with a student behind a closed door.
  - Never send children anywhere alone.
  - Never put a student in the hall or corner.
  - Never use standards as punishment (for example, writing "I will behave" 100 times).

Preparing for a Formal Evaluation

Being evaluated can sometimes be stressful, but with a supportive administrator, it can also be helpful. Formal evaluations can help you improve and polish your craft. During your first few years of teaching, you will no doubt be evaluated several times. Being prepared for these evaluations is essential.

CONSIDERATIONS

29
Formal
Evaluation
Checklist

- Before the day of the evaluation
  - Confirm expectations.
  - Find out what lesson plan format should be used.
  - Know which subject area will be observed.
  - Set up your first observation date, time, and lesson idea with the administrator at an initial planning meeting early in the year.
  - Ask other teachers for suggestions and for samples of submitted paperwork. Ask if there is a template.
  - Take into account the three types of learners—auditory, visual, and kinesthetic—when planning the lesson.
  - Submit all necessary paperwork, including the lesson plan.
  - Practice the lesson in advance so that you have your timing down, know that your equipment is working properly, and can confirm that all supplies are ready.
  - Share your lesson with a mentor or experienced teacher and ask for feedback.
  - Maintain all assessments, student portfolios, your grade book, and lesson plans.

- Day of the evaluation
  - Check the classroom environment for the following:
    - The floor is clean and free of debris.
    - The teacher's desk is neat and organized.
    - Students' desks are clean and organized.
    - Bookshelves and the class library are well organized.
    - The closet is organized and orderly.
    - Bulletin boards are appealing, show current student work with comments, include open-ended questions, and reflect focus standards.
    - Student portfolios are current and accessible.
    - The class schedule and content standards are posted in the room.
  - Present yourself well professionally: Dress appropriately, conduct yourself with confidence, and relax.
  - Have the lesson plan accessible and visible.
  - Organize all materials, equipment, and supplies to be used.
  - Walk through the lesson in your mind before you teach it.
  - Keep your voice low, and make sure that you don't do all the talking. Include the students' voices during instruction time.
  - Allow for wait time so that students can respond to questions.
- Follow-up
  - Keep current on all lesson planning and record keeping. Your administrator may make periodic visits and/or observations, and you should always be prepared.
  - Meet with your administrator for follow-up and for a signature on your evaluation.
  - Incorporate what you learn from the evaluation, and discuss and grow from the experience.

48, 49, 50
Lesson Plans

Teacher's Space

Lesson Planning

Lesson plans are critical to success in the classroom, and for you as a new teacher, they are absolutely imperative. Lesson plans should outline your instructional goals and activities for the week.

CONSIDERATIONS

- Keep up with your lesson planning.
- Avoid falling into a day-to-day lesson-planning trap.
- Plan at least one week in advance.
- Plan with a grade-level team or another teacher, if possible.
- Develop more than a single lesson for a given concept or standard.
- Think in terms of units, themes, and projects.
- Do long-range planning for units and themes.
- Consider a broad range of options for materials to include in your lesson plans, including the following:
  - Picture books
  - Videos and DVDs
  - Music
  - Equipment
  - Art supplies
- Prepare all materials in advance.
- Determine the lesson's objectives.
  - Align objectives to your state's standards.
  - Post lesson objectives.
  - Review lesson objectives with the students so they know what will be expected of them for the day, lesson, or unit.
- Use a variety of lesson components, which could include the following:
  - Opening or warm-up activities
  - Small group work
  - Whole class work
  - Individual work
- Refer to teacher's editions and curriculum guides to help you teach to the standards.
- Plan activities that provide for structured movement and discussion.

- Vary activities to address multiple learning styles, levels of ability, student interests, cultural considerations, and English Language Learner (ELL) needs.
- Take into account differentiation needs, materials, technology components, possible use of a teaching assistant, and any other relevant information that might help you make your lessons student-friendly and accessible for all.
- Establish clear expectations and objectives.
- Have a clear opening and closing.
- Structure your time. Be clear about how much time is required for each activity or lesson for the class period, subject area, or unit.
- Create an agenda or schedule, post it, and review it with the students so they know what will be expected of them for the day.
- Stay on track. Establish designated time allotments, and use a timer if necessary.
- Consider assessment. How will you monitor progress?
  - Observations
  - Finished product
  - Presentations
  - Rubric score
- Wrap up the class by having students summarize what they learned for that day or for that lesson.
- Follow up with purposeful homework that is an extension of concepts and activities included in the lesson.

22
Daily Schedule
Organizer

Teacher's Space

Record Keeping

Record keeping tracks your students' progress and provides evidence to support your grading decisions. Developing good record-keeping habits is essential for organizing, processing, and communicating the students' understanding of the curriculum.

CONSIDERATIONS

- Know what your school or district expects of you.
- Ask other teachers how they organize their grading.
- Grade in a way that works for you, making sure that students' graded assignments provide a well-rounded view of their progress.
- Handle your record keeping either as hard copy or electronically, depending on the requirements of your school or district.
- Track students' scores for exams, projects, and other assignments.
- Don't fall behind. Try to enter at least some scores every day or every week.
- Secure your grade book and/or your computer. Remember, student records are confidential.

Grade Book or Grading Program

A book specifically for recording grades or a grading program for tracking grades, assignments, and assessment scores makes record keeping much more efficient. This resource is usually provided for you by the school or district. If you are using a grade book, you can purchase it yourself, especially if you have a specific preference about which record-keeping tool you want to use.

CONSIDERATIONS

- Record, organize, and interpret students' assignments and assessments in your grade book or grading program on a regular basis.
- Set student goals based on performance.
- Use the grade book or grading program to support your teaching in many ways, including the following:
  - Providing evidence of student growth
  - Showing patterns of weakness or improvement
  - Helping you make informed decisions about students' progress

- Aiding discussions about students' progress with students, parents, and administrators
- Aiding explanations to parents about the progress their children are making and providing evidence to justify those claims
- Aiding referrals of students for special services
- Informing your own teaching practice and planning
- Helping you know what you need to reteach, when to move on, and when students have mastered certain subjects

Checklists

Checklists are an easy way to record scores, behavior, effort, and participation—all of which are part of the feedback provided on report cards and/or progress reports.

CONSIDERATIONS

64
Student
Evaluation Log

- Create specific checklists to reflect what you are looking for (for example, the material each individual student is learning or how individual students are behaving).
- Check items off as they are observed.

Anecdotal Notes

Anecdotal notes are helpful for fleshing out the quantitative information recorded in your grade book or grading program.

CONSIDERATIONS

- Use Post-it Notes for anecdotal notes (always include the date), and place them inside the appropriate subject portfolio for the student.
- Anecdotal notes can be accessed easily for conferencing with parents.

Class Record Charts

When displayed in the classroom, class record charts track similar information for all of your students. They can provide motivation for your students to complete or master the instructional material.

CONSIDERATIONS

- Use checks, stars, or stickers to indicate completion and/or mastery.
- Use a slash, X, circle, or empty cell to indicate non-completion and/or no mastery.
- Create a chart for each subject area and post it on the corresponding bulletin board.
- Use a variety of colored pens.
- In upper grades, appoint student monitors to maintain the charts.
- Cut up completed charts so that individual strips can be sent home for parents to see.

Teacher's Space

- Class record charts can be used to track many different activities, including the following:
  - Completed homework
  - Completion of assignments and/or mastery
  - Mastery of multiplication tables or other specific material

Subject Portfolios

66
Subject Portfolio

For subject areas such as math, social studies, science, and art, file folders can be set up to create student portfolios.

CONSIDERATIONS

- Establish guidelines for the subject area portfolios, such as the following:
  - Each portfolio must have three examples of the student's work.
  - Students select the graded assignments to place in their portfolios.
  - Students must write a note to explain why they selected a specific piece for their portfolio.
  - Students may replace items with improved examples of their work as they see fit.
  - Students must maintain neat and organized portfolios.
- Use these portfolios to support grade book or grading program records.
- Remember that portfolios are excellent items to display at Open House or to show to parents at conferences.

Writing Portfolios

80
Writing
Portfolio

Writing portfolios house a collection of students' writings.

CONSIDERATIONS

- Establish guidelines for writing portfolios, such as the following:
  - Each writing portfolio must have at least three examples of the student's work.
  - Students select which graded assignments to place in their writing portfolios.
  - Students may replace items with improved examples of their work as they see fit.
  - Students must maintain neat and organized writing portfolios.
- Discuss with each student their reason for selecting a particular writing assignment for inclusion in the writing portfolio and record the student's reason.
- Use these portfolios to support grade book or grading program records.
- Remember that portfolios are excellent items to display at Open House or to show to parents at conferences.

Assessment Folders

Assessment folders house a collection of assessments that monitor students' progress.

CONSIDERATIONS

- Keep all formal assessments in the students' assessment folders.
- Record assessment scores on the cover of each folder for easy access.
- Use assessment folders in conferences and during a referral process.
- Maintain these folders yourself; the contents are confidential.
- Have assessment folders accessible to administrators for review upon request.

63
Student
Assessment Log

Teacher's Space

New Teacher Reminders

As a new teacher, you must keep track of a tremendous amount of information. The following is a list of essentials to help you get off to a successful start.

CONSIDERATIONS

- Ask veteran teachers for guidance and advice throughout the year.
- Be aware of your credential expiration date and stay on top of renewal criteria.
- Get to know your union representative and your union rights. These representatives are very good sources of information, and they can answer most of your contract questions.
- Be on time for work, and be prepared. You are a professional now, and not only are you expected to be on time to work and to meetings, but you have a contract that requires it.
- Become familiar with school emergency procedures.
- Be careful about the snacks you give to students. Many children have allergies, such as to peanuts or dairy products. Ask parents at the beginning of the school year to inform you of any food allergies that their children have.
- Be aware of appropriate physical contact with students. A side hug, a high five, or a pat on the shoulder is okay.
- Never aggressively grab or hit a student.
- Never be alone with a student behind a closed door. In any situation where there might be a question about what is appropriate, keep your classroom door open.
- Start a professional portfolio of your work as a teacher. Keep it simple, and add to what you have already gathered from your work in the teacher preparation program.
- Don't bite off more than you can chew. This is your first year, and there will be many new things to learn. Work hard and do your best, but don't be too critical of yourself.

Teacher Portfolio

It is important that you start to develop a professional portfolio at the very beginning of your teaching career.

CONSIDERATIONS

- Keep a portfolio of your accomplishments as a teacher to demonstrate your abilities and readiness. It can be very important at several different points in your teaching career, including the following:
  - When changing schools or applying to a new school
  - When applying for a promotion as a coordinator or administrator
  - When applying for a grant or scholarship
- Keep your teacher portfolio up-to-date. It's important for it to be complete, and it can be hard to remember what you did a year ago if you need to catch up.
- Save all agendas. They provide evidence of professional developments and trainings that you have attended.
- Develop the portfolio as you go, and take your time with it.
- A professional portfolio might include the following:
  - Current credentials
  - Current résumé
  - Transcripts
  - Classroom assessments you have used, along with examples of related student work
  - Thematic units you have created
  - Special activities you have participated in at school
  - Professional developments you have presented
  - Positive evaluations from administrators
  - Grants you have written or received
  - Documentation of professional growth
  - Awards and accolades
  - Photos of projects
  - Video of projects

54
Professional
Development
Log

File Cabinet

Having a well-organized file cabinet that houses lessons, activities, and thematic units makes your job significantly easier.

CONSIDERATIONS

- Clean out your current file cabinets. Start fresh, and start clean.
- Keep only material that is current and relevant.
- Request file folders through your school. If your school doesn't provide them, purchase them yourself.
- Keep extra file folders on hand.
- As you acquire new items, label and file them in a way that makes sense to you (for example, "CVC Words," "Multiplication").
- Determine which method of organizing your file cabinet is best for you—for example, in alphabetical order, by month, by time of year, by theme, or by need.

Files

- Instructional and/or curriculum files
  - Assessments by subject area (math, spelling, science, etc.)
  - Book report templates
  - Holiday units, worksheets, and activities
  - Science experiments
  - Subject-related worksheets (math, grammar, spelling, etc.)
  - Theme and unit plans

12, 13
Book Reports

- Professional files
  - Parent newsletters, including weekly or monthly copies
  - Parent correspondence, including the welcome letter and Back to School Night invitation
  - Office memos about future events and meetings
  - Students' report cards and progress reports (or copies of them)
  - Substitute teacher folder, including both information for a substitute teacher and contact information for reliable substitutes
  - Evaluations
- School files
  - Notes and/or excuses from home for absences and tardies
  - Agendas for all in-service and professional developments
- Student files
  - Individual student folders containing records of anecdotal notes and notes to yourself about a student's behavior and/or progress
  - Student information, including emergency contact information, health concerns, Individualized Education Plan (IEP) considerations, and English Language Development (ELD) levels

53
Newsletter
(sample, blank)
79
Welcome Letter
(sample, blank)
04
Back to School
Night Invitation

School Culture

Like any place of employment, a school has its own distinct culture, dependent on the different personalities of the many individuals who are part of it. Those personalities and the division of leadership roles among them create a unique school dynamic. Getting to know the school's culture takes time.

CONSIDERATIONS

- Have a positive attitude.
- Keep a smile on your face.
- Give everyone a chance; judge for yourself.
- Try to introduce yourself to all the teachers and staff members in the school.
- Take your time settling into a school. Your first year as a teacher should be focused on your classroom.
- Don't bring your personal life to work. Leave your personal life at the door, and come into your classroom ready to teach.
- Take your time deciding whom you choose to get to know at school and to what extent.
- Try to get to know the teachers next door and across the hall from you. Proximity makes them easily accessible to you, and they can be great resources of information and advice.
- Avoid school gossip. Focus on the classroom and instruction.
- Don't take on too much, such as committee work, a graduate degree, or professional development classes, until you are comfortable at your job. During your first year, remember that less is more.
- Be prepared to say "no." Many new teachers take on too many extra responsibilities. You are not required to say "yes" to everything.
- Conduct yourself appropriately as a teacher. Make sure that you in no way jeopardize your credentials. When in doubt, ask your union representative for advice.
- Ask veteran teachers for help. They know what your are facing, because they were once new teachers themselves.

Acronyms and Terms

Acronyms are commonly used in educational settings. Many grants, special programs, designated groups of students, laws, and standardized tests have names that are commonly shortened into acronyms. Knowing these can help you navigate the system.

- **AB**—Assembly Bill
- **ADA**—Average Daily Attendance
- **ADD**—Attention Deficit Disorder
- **ADHD**—Attention Deficit Hyperactive Disorder
- **AIP**—Academic Improvement Plan
- **AP**—Advanced Placement; Assistant Principal
- **APE**—Adaptive PE
- **API**—Academic Performance Index
- **AYP**—Adequate Yearly Progress; Academic Yearly Plan
- **BCLAD**—Bilingual Cross-cultural Language and Academic Development
- **BTSA**—Beginning Teacher Support and Assessment
- **CLAD**—Cross-cultural Language and Academic Development
- **COLA**—Cost of Living Adjustment
- **CPS**—Child Protective Services
- **EELA**—Elementary English Language Arts
- **EL**—English Language
- **ELD**—English Language Development
- **ELL**—English Language Learner
- **ELPT**—English Language Proficiency Test
- **ESL**—English as a Second Language
- **GATE**—Gifted and Talented Education
- **IDEA**—Individuals with Disabilities Education Act
- **IEP**—Individualized Education Plan
- **ILO**—Intended Learning Outcome
- **LCSW**—Licensed Clinical Social Worker
- **LD**—Learning Disability

- **LEA**—Local Education Agency
- **LH**—Learning Handicapped
- **NCLB**—No Child Left Behind Act
- **NEA**—National Education Association
- **PD**—Professional Development
- **PEP**—Personalized Education Plan
- **PI**—Program Improvement
- **PTA**—Parent Teacher Association
- **PTSA**—Parent Teacher Student Association
- **RSP**—Resource Specialist Program
- **SAC**—School Advisory Committee
- **SAT**—Scholastic Achievement Test
- **SAT/Stanford 9**—Stanford Achievement Test
- **SDC**—Special Day Class
- **SEA**—State Education Agency
- **SED/ED**—Severely Emotionally Disturbed/Emotionally Disturbed
- **SEI**—Structured English Instruction/Sheltered English Instruction
- **SEP**—Student Education Plan
- **SH**—Severely Handicapped
- **SIP**—School Improvement Plan
- **SLD**—Specific Learning Disability
- **SST**—Student Study Team
- **STAR**—Standardized Testing and Reporting
- **STRS**—State Teacher Retirement System
- **TESOL**—Teaching English to Speakers of Other Languages
- **TE**—Teacher's Edition (of any curricular program)
- **Title I**—Financial Assistance to Local Educational Agencies for the Education of Children of Low-Income Families
- **Title III**—Language Instruction for Limited English Proficient and Immigrant Students

In Case You're Out: Preparing for a Substitute Teacher

There are times when every teacher needs to be out of the classroom. Illness, family emergencies, personal necessity, trainings, and meetings can keep you from your daily teaching routine. Absences may be a single day, or they may extend to several days. In any case, you need to be prepared so that a substitute teacher can continue with your daily routine in the classroom.

CONSIDERATIONS

- District and/or school policy on absences
  - Know your allotted number of sick days per year.
  - Know how to arrange for a substitute.
- Arranging for a substitute early
  - Use the district's substitute teacher finder (by telephone or online).
  - Notify the office as early as possible that you have arranged for a substitute.
- Emergency substitute plans
  - Include typical review activities so that your students aren't thrown off in your absence.
  - Cover all curricular areas.
  - Include one to two days of plans, just in case.
- Discussing your absence with your students
  - Talk with your students prior to your absence, if possible.
  - Review your expectations for their behavior.
  - Discuss how your students can and should support the substitute teacher.

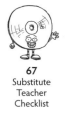

67
Substitute
Teacher
Checklist

- Notifications
  - Notify the office.
  - Notify other grade-level team members.
  - Update your class website so that parents know that you'll be absent.
- Support for the substitute
  - Provide your personal cell phone number and e-mail address for the substitute so that you can be contacted if necessary.
  - If you will not be available, provide contact information (phone number, e-mail address) for a grade-level teacher or teachers you trust.
  - Provide the substitute with the room number of a friendly, helpful grade-level teacher.
  - Provide the names of responsible and reliable students.
  - Let selected staff members know you'll be absent (for example, an aide or a resource teacher).
- Preparation for the substitute
  - Develop detailed and organized lesson plans.
  - Supply necessary copies, materials, teacher manuals, teacher's editions, and other resource books.
  - Leave your classroom clean, orderly, and ready.
  - Include a current seating chart so that students' names are available, and set up student name plates on the desks.
  - Provide the duty schedule and class schedule for the day.
  - Note any special schedules or activities for the day.
  - Make sure the emergency exit procedure and the emergency backpack are clearly visible.
  - Provide a copy of your classroom rules and consequences.
  - Have referral forms and hall passes available for the substitute.
  - Make sure that there are enough sharpened pencils in the classroom.
  - Confirm that all necessary supplies are available.
  - Provide a list of classroom helpers.
- Policies
  - Explain restroom breaks.
  - Explain water breaks.
  - Explain pencil sharpening rules.
  - Explain food and drink acceptability.
  - Discuss use of cell phones and electronics.
- Equipping the substitute
  - Develop lists of "must do" and "may do" requirements for student work.
  - Have a designated place for extra activity sheets: When you make copies of a worksheet, copy a few extras to keep in an "extra work" basket.

69
Substitute
Teacher
Information

68
Substitute
Teacher
Feedback

- Strategies
  - Emergency substitute planning—being ready with a complete set of lesson plans with activities that span the curriculum, including all relevant and necessary information
  - Week-ahead planning—completing lesson plans for the following week by taking a little time every day after school to develop them. A weekly plan could include the following:
    - *Monday*: Complete language arts plans and make copies for a week's worth of activities.
    - *Tuesday*: Complete math plans and make copies for a week's worth of activities.
    - *Wednesday*: Complete other curricular area planning (science, social studies, health, art, PE, etc.) and make copies for a week's worth of activities.
    - *Thursday*: Clean and organize the classroom.
    - *Friday*: Leave all plans and copies at your desk so that they are available for the following week, whether it is you or a substitute who is in the classroom.

48, 49, 50
Lesson Plans

75, 76
Weekly Lesson Overviews

77
Weekly Lesson Plan Overview

78
Weekly Lesson Plans

Teacher's Space

Bilingual Overview

Each year, it is more and more likely that you will have students in your class whose primary language is not English. These students are often categorized as English Language Learners (ELLs) and are required to receive English language instruction.

CONSIDERATIONS

- Ask if the school and/or district already has a specific ELL plan in place for you to use.
- Ask about supported curriculum that has already been adopted.
- Create a progress system to track students' language development.
- Locate or create appropriate assessments to use in promoting students out of the English Language Development (ELD) program.
- Check with administrators and other teachers from your school for guidelines and strategies.

Common Acronyms and Terms in a Bilingual Program

ELD—English Language Development
ELL—English Language Learner
ESL—English as a Second Language
SDAIE—Specifically Designed Academic Instruction in English
SIOP—Sheltered Instruction Observation Protocol
Comprehensible Input—Information delivered so that it is understandable at a given ELD level

Strategies for Working with English Language Learners

SDAIE (Specifically Designed Academic Instruction in English)

SDAIE is strategic instruction that layers (scaffolds) lessons to review vocabulary and concepts according to a student's needs.

- SDAIE targets and narrows a lesson's focus, making it easier and more appropriate for the English language learner's comprehensible input.
- SDAIE is a strategy useful for all learners.

Realia (Part of SDAIE)

- Realia uses tangible items to introduce vocabulary or concepts.
- Students use any or all of their five senses with the Realia strategy.

Preteach/Reteach (Part of SDAIE)

- Preteach/Reteach involves preteaching the vocabulary or concepts of a lesson.
- Preteach/Reteach involves reteaching concepts for reinforcement purposes after the original teaching of the lesson.
- Familiarity and background knowledge are increased with the Preteach/Reteach strategy.

TPR (Total Physical Response)/Role-Play (Part of SDAIE)

- Total Physical Response (TPR) involves physically performing actions that are described in words.
- Role-playing helps demonstrate key words and key concepts for new information.

Pictures/Graphic Organizers (Part of SDAIE)

- Picture cues are established for rules, vocabulary, historical references, people, etc.
- Graphic organizers help simplify topics for writing purposes.

Teacher's Space

English Language Development (ELD) Levels

There are five levels of English Language Development instruction. Delivery of lessons is often differentiated in terms of meeting the needs of students at their ELD level. These levels help explain students' language capabilities. The goal is for the student to move up at least one ELD level per year, eventually being designated as a fluent English speaker.

The following is a simplified look at each ELD level. Students would communicate as follows if engaged in a lesson:

- **ELD 1**
  - Responding nonverbally or using only a few words
  - Pointing to pictures in order to respond
  - Drawing pictures related to the topic
- **ELD 2**
  - Giving verbal responses of a few words
  - Using "yes" and "no" responses appropriately
  - Writing phrases with invented spelling
- **ELD 3**
  - Giving verbal responses in short phrases, often omitting words such as verbs
  - Responding to "why"
  - Being able to elaborate
  - Writing phrases or simple sentences (Conventional spelling begins.)
- **ELD 4**
  - Conversing verbally with few errors
  - Answering during class discussions
  - Writing related sentences that have strong vocabulary and few errors
- **ELD 5**
  - Responding verbally like a native speaker
  - Having discussions like a native speaker
  - Writing with the ease of a native speaker

Teacher Resources

Teacher resources—books on curriculum and instruction, methodologies, or true story accounts—help develop your craft as an educator. All of these can inspire you to do and be your best as an educator.

CONSIDERATIONS

- Use teacher resources to do any and all of the following:
  - Keep you current on changes in the field of education
  - Assist you in becoming a lifelong learner
  - Give you innovative and interesting ideas
  - Help you deliver engaging curriculum
  - Assist you in managing your classroom
  - Inspire you
  - Motivate you
  - Help you set reasonable goals and expectations for all of your students
- Purchase resources from any of several sources.
  - Online at websites such as half.com, Amazon.com, and barnesandnoble.com
  - At local teacher supply stores
  - At major bookstores
  - At university bookstores
- Search out used textbooks to save money.
- Check out resources from a local library. Many of the recommended resources are available at public libraries.
- Borrow resources from other teachers or from your administrator.

15 Top Resources for Teachers

Cohen, Brad and Lisa Wysocky. *Front of the Class: How Tourette Syndrome Made Me the Teacher I Never Had.* 2008. (ISBN 9780312571399)

> *Front of the Class* is about Tourette syndrome, but it's also a touching account of the difficulties and triumphs in one young man's life that can be applied to students who have a learning disorder, chronic disease, or any situation that makes them different from their peers.

Delpit, Lisa and Herbert Kohl. *Other People's Children: Cultural Conflict in the Classroom.* 2006. (ISBN 9781595580740)

> Children of color and poor children—"other people's children"—are often victimized by school administrators and others who see "damaged and dangerous caricatures" instead of able youngsters who are capable of learning in a mainstream setting. Delpit discusses her views on teaching African American children, based on professional research and her own experience of school as an alien environment.

Esquith, Rafe. *Teach Like Your Hair's on Fire: The Methods and Madness Inside Room 56.* 2007. (ISBN 9780143112860)

> In his Los Angeles public school classroom, Rafe Esquith helps impoverished immigrant children become happy, self-confident people. This account of his work provides teachers and parents with the techniques, exercises, and innovations that have made its author popular.

Freedom Writers, Zlata Filipovic, and Erin Gruwell. *The Freedom Writers Diary: How a Teacher and 150 Teens Used Writing to Change Themselves and the World Around Them.* 1999. (ISBN 9780385494229)

> As a young English teacher at Wilson High School in Long Beach, California, Gruwell and her at-risk students undertake a life-changing, eye-opening journey against intolerance and misunderstanding. With powerful entries from the students' own diaries and a narrative text by Gruwell, *The Freedom Writers Diary* is an uplifting account of how hard work, courage, and the spirit of determination change the lives of a teacher and her students.

Gruwell, Erin. *The Freedom Writers Diary Teacher's Guide.* 2007. (ISBN 9780767926966)

> Designed for educators by the teacher who created *The Freedom Writers*, this standards-based teacher's guide includes innovative teaching techniques that engage, empower, and enlighten.

Johnson, LouAnne. *Teaching Outside the Box: How to Grab Your Students by Their Brains.* 2005. (ISBN 9780787974718)

> *Teaching Outside the Box* offers tangible strategies that can help teachers create engaging classroom environments where students want to learn and teachers enjoy teaching—using "outside the box" approaches.

Jones, Fredric H., Patrick Jones, Jo Lynn, and Fred Jones. *Fred Jones Tools for Teaching: Discipline, Instruction, Motivation.* 2007. (ISBN 9780965026321)

> Fred Jones offers tools for developing discipline, instruction, and motivation in your students with the goal of reducing the stress of teaching. He includes tips to help you reduce disruptions, disrespectful talk, overuse of hand raising, and wasted time.

McBride, James. *The Color of Water.* 1996. (ISBN 9781594481925)

Kids who come from diverse backgrounds have a noticeable desire to identify who they are and where they come from. *The Color of Water* introduces a man whose mother was white and whose father was black. The two stories he tells, his mother's and his own, describe a biracial family that succeeded and achieved the American dream—socially and academically—despite the obstacles placed in its way by society.

Mooney, Jonathan. *The Short Bus: A Journey Beyond Normal.* 2007. (ISBN 9780805088045)

Children with physical, mental, and learning disabilities often ride a "short bus" to school, which signals that they are different. Mooney was one of those short-bus children because he was dyslexic. After he graduated from Brown University, he co-wrote a book on learning disabilities and began speaking publicly on the subject. Then he set out on a journey: He bought an old short bus, and he traveled from Los Angeles to Maine to Washington and back to Los Angeles, stopping to visit with people he met along the way who were also "not normal."

Mortenson, Greg and David Oliver Relin. *Three Cups of Tea: One Man's Mission to Promote Peace . . . One School at a Time.* 2007. (ISBN 9780143038252)

Greg Mortenson's promise to build the first school in the impoverished Pakistani village of Korphe grew into the Central Asia Institute, which has since constructed more than 50 schools across rural Pakistan and Afghanistan. His inspiring story will make you ask, "What else can *I* do?"

Pink, Daniel H. *A Whole New Mind: Why Right-Brainers Will Rule the Future.* 2006. (ISBN 9781594481710)

Pink discusses a future that belongs to a different kind of person with a different kind of mind: designers, inventors, teachers, storytellers, and creative and empathic "right-brain" thinkers.

Springer, Steve, Brandy Alexander, and Kimberly Persiani-Becker. *The Organized Teacher: A Hands-On Guide to Setting Up and Running a Terrific Classroom.* 2005. (ISBN 9780071457071)

The Organized Teacher provides advice on everything from desk arrangement to unit planning, sample room setups to behavior-management strategies, and practical advice on creating student portfolios, checklists, and scoring rubrics.

Springer, Steve, Brandy Alexander, and Kimberly Persiani-Becker. *The Creative Teacher: An Encyclopedia of Ideas to Energize Your Curriculum.* 2006. (ISBN 9780071472807)

The Creative Teacher offers inventive tools to enhance standards-based curricula and helpful strategies for creating new and engaging lesson plans. It is filled with ideas for everything from bulletin boards to math activities.

Teacher's Space

Springer, Steve, Brandy Alexander, and Kimberly Persiani-Becker. *The Festive Teacher: Multicultural Activities for Your Curriculum*. 2008. (ISBN 9780071492638)

> Take holidays to the next level by incorporating their historical and cultural significance into your lesson plans. *The Festive Teacher* includes activities and story starters that are directly connected to holidays and standard curricula.

Thompson, J. *First Year Teacher's Survival Guide: Ready-to-Use Strategies, Tools & Activities for Meeting the Challenges of Each School Day*. 2007. (ISBN 9780787994556)

> *First Year Teacher's Survival Guide* gives teachers a variety of strategies, activities, and tools for creating a positive learning environment. Included are useful tips for being a team player and connecting with students while handling behavior problems and working within diverse classrooms.

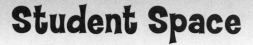

EAST
Student Space

The East side of the room is dedicated to the students and their space—both within the classroom and outside it. In planning the layout and materials for your classroom, it is important to create a student-centered space that offers students a chance to play and learn independently.

In this section, we assist you in setting up and managing your classroom to provide students with a rich environment that lends itself to exploration and learning. In addition to the general classroom environment, we discuss the classroom library, the computer center, and bulletin boards. Planning interesting, fun, and student-centered field trips related to the content standards for your grade level is also addressed. Because no classroom is successful without management, this section includes conflict resolution strategies for students so that they can learn to manage conflicts without immediately seeking teacher support.

Look for help with the following:

Classroom Library

A library is an important component of the classroom for your students. It takes time to build a classroom library, but once developed, it will be an excellent resource for both you and your students.

CONSIDERATIONS

- Find books for free or for purchase at some or all of the following sources:
  - Friends whose children have outgrown them
  - Other teachers
  - Yard sales
  - Obsolete library books
  - Book fair events
  - Monthly book order clubs
  - Grants
- Designate an area of the classroom where students can choose a book and read.
- Create a comfortable reading space with bookshelves, a rug, large pillows or a beanbag chair, and even a teddy bear or two.
- Organize books by theme or genre—in plastic tubs for lower grades and on shelves for upper grades.
- Label book covers with your name and room number, using a permanent marker.
- Create book placeholders so that when a student has pulled a book out to read, the book placeholder can hold its spot on the shelf.
- Establish a system for checking out books so that students can sign out books to read at home.

51
Library
Sign-Out Sheet

12, 13
Book Reports

55
Readng Log

- Assign book reports.
  - Students select books to report on.
  - Students in lower grades can transport books home in a large plastic zipper bag or a large laminated manila envelope.
  - Students keep books for a weekend, a week, or another time period that you establish.
  - Students complete the appropriate book report form.
  - Students track their reading using a monthly reading log.
- Organize books by theme or genre, using a classification system such as one of the following:
  - General—Science, Social Science, Math
  - Theme—Plants, Friendship, Courage, Multicultural, Favorite Authors
  - Standards—Plate Tectonics, Volcanoes
- For students in lower grades, identify a book's level with a colored sticker on the book cover, using a system such as the following:
  - Green = Easy
  - Yellow = Intermediate
  - Red = Advanced

Selecting Books

CONSIDERATIONS

- Visit a bookstore and spend time with picture books if you are unfamiliar with them.
- Select books that inspire you and that you think your students will enjoy.
- Include a variety of authors and genres for picture books.
- Include rich, multicultural books.
- Consider varied reading levels.
- Think beyond books—include magazines and comic books.

RECOMMENDATIONS

- Alma Flor Ada (Grades K–4): Latino children and families
  Dear Peter Rabbit
  Gathering the Sun: An Alphabet in Spanish and English
  The Gold Coin
  I Love Saturdays y domingos
  Mamá Goose: A Latino Nursery Treasury
  My Name Is María Isabel
  ¡Pío Peep! Traditional Spanish Nursery Rhymes
  Tales Our Abuelitas Told: A Hispanic Folktale Collection

- Francisco X. Alarcón (Grades K–6): Latino children and families
  Angels Ride Bikes and Other Fall Poems /
    Los ángeles andan en bicicleta y otros poemas de otoño
  Animal Poems of the Iguazú / Animalario del Iguazú
  From the Bellybutton of the Moon and Other Summer Poems /
    Del ombligo de la luna y otros poemas de verano
  Iguanas in the Snow and Other Winter Poems /
    Iguanas en la nieve y otros poemas de invierno
  Laughing Tomatoes and Other Spring Poems /
    Jitomates Risueños y otros poemas de primavera
  Poems to Dream Together / Poemas para soñar juntos
- Eric Carle (Grades Pre-K-3): Science-related easy readers, repetition
  All in a Day
  Brown Bear, Brown Bear, What Do You See?
  Chip Has Many Brothers
  The Foolish Tortoise
  The Grouchy Ladybug
  A House for Hermit Crab
  Mister Seahorse
  The Mixed-Up Chameleon
  Pancakes, Pancakes!
  The Tiny Seed
  The Very Busy Spider
  The Very Clumsy Click Beetle
  The Very Hungry Caterpillar
  The Very Lonely Firefly
  Walter the Baker
- Mem Fox (Grades K–3): Rhythm and rhyme
  Harriet, You'll Drive Me Wild!
  Hattie and the Fox
  Koala Lou
  Night Noises
  Possum Magic
  Shoes from Grandpa
  Sleepy Bears
  Wilfrid Gordon McDonald Partridge
  Wombat Divine
  Zoo-Looking

- Gerald McDermott (Grades 2–6): Trickster tales from various continents
    Anansi the Spider: A Tale from the Ashanti
    Arrow to the Sun: A Pueblo Indian Tale
    Coyote: A Trickster Tale from the American Southwest
    Creation
    Jabutí the Tortoise: A Trickster Tale from the Amazon
    Papagayo: The Mischief Maker
    Pig-Boy: A Trickster Tale from Hawai'i
    Raven: A Trickster Tale from the Pacific Northwest
    The Stonecutter: A Japanese Folk Tale
    Zomo the Rabbit: A Trickster Tale from West Africa
- Pat Mora (Grades K–5): Multicultural, family-related stories
    Agua, Agua, Agua
    A Birthday Basket for Tía
    Confeti: Poemas para niños
    Confetti: Poems for Children
    The Desert Is My Mother / El desierto es mi madre
    Doña Flor: A Tall Tale About a Giant Woman with a Great Big Heart
    Let's Eat! / ¡A comer!
    A Library for Juana: The World of Sor Juana Inés
    Una biblioteca para Juana: El mundo de Sor Juana Inés
    Listen to the Desert / Oye al desierto
    Love to Mamá: A Tribute to Mothers
    Maria Paints the Hills
    The Rainbow Tulip
    Tomás and the Library Lady
    Tomás y la señora de la biblioteca
- Jack Prelutsky (Grades K–6): Silly poems about everyday life
    For Laughing Out Loud: Poems to Tickle Your Funnybone
    The Frogs Wore Red Suspenders
    If Not for the Cat
    It's Raining Pigs & Noodles
    A Pizza the Size of the Sun
    Pizza, Pigs, and Poetry: How to Write a Poem
    Poetry Fun by the Ton with Jack Prelutsky
    The Random House Book of Poetry for Children
    Ride a Purple Pelican
    What a Day It Was at School!

- Dr. Seuss (Grades K–6): Life-affirming themes, rhythm and rhyme
  Did I Ever Tell You How Lucky You Are?
  Horton Hears a Who!
  The Lorax
  Oh Say Can You Say?
  Oh, the Places You'll Go!
  Oh, the Thinks You Can Think!
  One Fish Two Fish Red Fish Blue Fish
  The Cat in the Hat
  The Shape of Me and Other Stuff
  The Sneetches and Other Stories
- Shel Silverstein (Grades K–6): Silly everyday poems and stories
  Don't Bump the Glump!: And Other Fantasies
  Falling Up
  A Giraffe and a Half
  The Giving Tree
  Lafcadio, the Lion Who Shot Back
  A Light in the Attic
  The Missing Piece
  The Missing Piece Meets the Big O
  Runny Babbit: A Billy Sook
  Where the Sidewalk Ends
  Who Wants a Cheap Rhinoceros?
- Other authors to consider in developing your multicultural library
  Arnold Adoff
  Yangsook Choi
  Paul Goble
  Virginia Hamilton
  Florence Parry Heide
  Karen Hesse
  Naomi Shihab Nye
  Patricia Pollaco
  Allen Say
  John Steptoe
  Michele Maria Surat
  Mildred D. Taylor
  Laurence Yep

Bulletin Boards

Bulletin boards showcase your students' work and demonstrate the learning that is taking place within your classroom.

CONSIDERATIONS

- Keep bulletin boards clean and organized.
- Remember that bulletin boards are often the first thing people look for when entering your classroom: They are the first impression of the classroom, its organization, and the instruction that takes place there.
- Try to display at least one or two samples of work for each student, because this gives all the students ownership of the classroom and builds a sense of pride.
- Keep bulletin boards current—try to update a different bulletin board every couple of weeks.
- Represent a variety of subject areas and themes on your bulletin boards.
- If you have a limited number of boards available, consider dividing the bulletin boards in half to make it possible for you to display student work in all of the subject areas.
- Represent each student's best work (regardless of score).
- Keep student work as the primary focus of the classroom's bulletin boards. A busy background can distract the focus from student work.
- Pay attention to detail.

Bulletin Board Elements

Every bulletin board should include several components beyond the background and borders, including most if not all of the following:

* Background
* Colorful border
* Title
* Student work with written teacher feedback and/or rubric score
* Content standards being addressed
* Question
* Scoring rubric
* List of key words
* Teacher example

Background

* Coordinate colors.
* Keep it simple; eliminate distracting elements.
* Choose a background color you can live with; it may be up all year.
* Prepare the background for your bulletin board as follows:
  * Mount the background first; then add the borders.
  * Measure the background material, adding a little bit extra just to make sure, and use push pins to attach it to the board.
  * Start in one corner, and staple the material in that corner. Use a yardstick to pull the material tight, flattening it as you work your way across the board, and stapling the material at regular intervals.
  * With a pair of scissors, cut off any extra material at the edges (small gaps will be covered by the border). Remove the push pins.
* Materials appropriate for the background include the following:
  * Paper
    * Butcher paper—usually available at the school site in a variety of colors, can fade over time, needs to be changed each year
    * Fadeless paper—purchase from a teacher supply store, excellent, lasts for years
    * Recycled paper (newspaper, magazines, construction paper scraps, grocery bags, old charts, book jackets, maps, any paper that can be recycled for this purpose)—can be collaged onto a bulletin board, more labor-intensive, can be visually busy
  * Cloth
    * Cloth or bed sheets with a subject-specific pattern (for example, numbers, planets, dinosaurs, fossils)
    * Burlap—usually available at the school site
    * Felt—usually available at the school site

Border

- Coordinate the border with the background color, whether the border is a solid color or a pattern.
- Consider borders that are theme-based and age-appropriate (for example, numbers for math).
- Purchase border materials at a teacher supply store or online.
- Students can create borders that are theme-related using sentence strips. (One pack of sentence strips per bulletin board is more than enough.)
- Be creative, and have fun choosing the borders.
- Make sure it works for you: You will have to live with it.
- Select background and border combinations that can stay up all year if possible, because that means one less thing for you to worry about as a new teacher.
- Prepare the border for your bulletin board as follows:
  - Use push pins to place the border pieces around the bulletin board.
  - Match up the design neatly: Attention to detail will make your boards pop!
  - Staple the border pieces in place. Remove the push pins.
- Materials appropriate for the border include the following:
  - Purchased border
    - Solid colors
    - Theme-related
    - Age-appropriate
  - Recycled materials
  - Cloth border, fringe, large buttons, piping
  - Subject-related (printed images from the Internet, possibly brought in by students)
  - Die cuts based on the board's theme (for example, pumpkins, snowflakes, numbers, letters of the alphabet, groundhogs; a die-cut machine is available at most schools)
  - Old game cards
  - Postcards, holiday cards
  - Collectible cards such as baseball cards

Student Work

- Select work that students are proud of.
- Make sure that students understand their score on the displayed work, as well as the rubric for it.
- Write comments on the student work: Mention something to improve, and follow that with something positive.
- Assign a grade.

- Try to represent each student on at least one of the bulletin boards in your classroom.
- Present your students' best work, but realize that the scores don't have to be perfect.
- Prepare the student work for display on your bulletin board as follows:
  - Select border paper for the pieces of student work to be displayed. Construction paper works fine, but it may need to be trimmed.
    - Coordinate the color of this border paper with the main bulletin board background and border.
    - Cut the border paper to size so that an even border will show around each piece of student work.
  - Use push pins to attach the border papers, spacing them out evenly and symmetrically across the bulletin board.
    - Try to fit as many border papers on the bulletin board as possible, so that you can have as much student work displayed as possible.
    - Staple the border papers to the bulletin board. Remove the push pins.
  - Select student work to be displayed.
  - Score the work and write comments on it.
  - Mount the student work to the border papers that have been stapled to the bulletin board.
    - Use push pins to mount the student work. This allows you to easily switch out the pieces of the students' work, while leaving the border papers in place.

Content Standards, Question, and Rubric

CONSIDERATIONS

- Rephrase the content standards and objectives in child-friendly language, selecting the specific standard or objective that supports your outcome.
- Select a question that is open-ended (for example, a question that elicits a thoughtful response rather than a "yes" or "no" answer); use words like "how" and "why."
- Post a rubric that breaks down your rationale for the full range of scores:
  - 4—All goals achieved
  - 3—Most goals achieved
  - 2—Some goals achieved
  - 1—Minimal goals achieved

58, 59, 60, 61
Rubrics

- Prepare the content standard and question for display on your bulletin board by writing the standard and question on sentence strips. (Print them for students in grades K through 2; write them in cursive for students in grades 3 through 6.)
- Use push pins to mount and hold these items in place to make it easier to switch them out when appropriate.
- Plan the overall bulletin board layout to include these items.

Organization by Subject Area and Theme

- Subject areas
  - Math
  - Reading
  - Spelling
  - Writing
  - Social Studies
  - Science
  - Health
  - Art
- Themes
  - Holidays (for example, Halloween, Christmas)
  - History (for example, civil rights)
  - Practical application (for example, cooking with fractions)
  - Historical figures (for example, timelines)
  - Science (for example, biomes, weather)
  - Reading (for example, book covers)

Supplementing Bulletin Boards with Three-Dimensional Art

CONSIDERATIONS

- Remember that student work is the primary focus; don't go overboard with supplemental art objects.
- Have a display table in front of the bulletin board with artifacts that relate to the theme.
- Add supplemental art after the bulletin board is complete; place it around the student work.
- Determine if the art objects really support and enhance the bulletin board (it can be messy).
- Three-dimensional art could include the following:
  - Multiple colors of folded, twisted, or crinkled butcher paper
  - Styrofoam plates, cups, and trays that can be cut and sculpted
  - Natural items, such as leaves, sticks, dried flowers, and branches
  - Cheap plastic toys (for example, spiders, skeletons, eggs, and cars)
  - Pipe cleaners, yarn, cord (usually available at the school site)
  - Velcro (for mounting larger objects)
  - Balloons
  - Streamers
  - Craft supplies (for example, googly eyes, cotton balls, and beads)

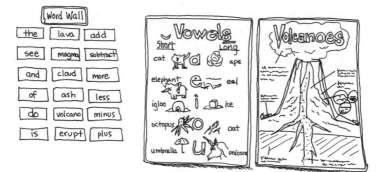

Classroom Walls, Posters, and Charts

Your classroom environment should be strategically planned with the ultimate goal of learning in mind. There is a real art to creating a dynamic classroom environment—one that supports learning, is fun and engaging, and yet is neat, orderly, and purposeful. However, you don't have to be an artist to provide an appealing space for your students.

CONSIDERATIONS

- Check with the school office for the policy on hanging posters and charts on the walls. What is—or, more important, what isn't—allowed?
- Sticky putty is an excellent way to hang posters without leaving a residue or ruining the paint.
- Purchase grade-level–appropriate charts and posters to display on the walls and closet doors (if allowed).
- Have students work in cooperative groups to create theme-based posters for display on the walls (for example, erupting volcanoes, the water cycle, the rainforest, the food pyramid).

Word Walls

A word wall is a chart or poster with specific words that relate to and support learning of a particular skill or content area. They can be powerful learning tools in the classroom.

CONSIDERATIONS

- Use word walls as living and interactive tools for learning.
- Encourage students to actively engage with word walls.
  - Introduce new words of the week.
  - Build on students' understanding of how words work.

- Use word walls as a reference for current units being studied.
- Use word walls during writing projects as a primary spelling resource.
- Have several ongoing word walls in the classroom, each with a different focus, including the following:
  - Weekly spelling words
  - Seasonal words
  - Key vocabulary for a theme or unit
  - Word study (for example, verbs, adjectives, compound words, editing rules)
- Types of organization for word walls could include the following:
  - **Pocket chart**—Use words for spelling, vocabulary, word study for the week, or a theme or unit. Write the words on index "word" cards. This allows you to change them, move them around, and turn them over.
  - **Chart paper**— To develop the list, write relevant words on chart paper as students make suggestions. These words can be used for a specific time period (a day, a week, a month) or for as long as you're working with a certain theme. The word wall can be stored and revisited throughout the year.
  - **Bulletin board**—Designate an entire bulletin board for use as a word wall (or perhaps multiple smaller word walls). Words can be added to this word wall throughout the school year. Each new word can be a permanent addition, or early words can be replaced with new additions as students master the words.

Student-Created Posters

For a powerful cooperative group activity, groups of two to four students work together to create posters for display in the classroom.

CONSIDERATIONS

- List the desired components for students to include in their posters (that is, establish a rubric).
- Discuss design and layout with the class.
- Have students get approval of a newsprint mock-up of the poster before they create the final poster on good paper.
- Have students in lower grades use crayons.
- Have students in upper grades use colored pencils for small detailed areas and markers for larger areas.
- Display posters to create a student-centered classroom environment.

Multicultural Posters

The world is gradually becoming smaller because of cell phones, the Internet, and other technological advances. Therefore, providing exposure to different cultures is a critical part of education today.

CONSIDERATIONS

- Purchase multicultural posters at teacher supply stores and bookstores.
- Display the covers of select multicultural books that you have available.
- Have students create posters that tell who they are and where they come from to demonstrate the diversity present in your classroom.
- Recognize all students in your classroom, including students of both genders, students with special needs as well as those without special needs, and students of every national, ethnic, and cultural background represented in your class.
- Culturally themed months during the school year could include the following:
  - Hispanic Heritage Month
  - Black History Month

Subject-Related Posters

Posters that relate to specific subject goals can serve as resources for students.

CONSIDERATIONS

- Purchase posters online and at teacher supply stores.
- Have cooperative groups of two to four students make subject-related posters. This adds a personal touch to the unit and solidifies learning.
- Reference specific points included on the posters when moving through a unit of study.
- Remind students that illustrations should be a part of any poster they create.
- Use student-created posters as an assessment of how well concepts have been understood and information learned.

Tracking Progress and Mastery

Charts and posters can be used to creatively track student progress and mastery in many areas.

63
Student
Assessment Log

64
Student
Evaluation Log

CONSIDERATIONS

- Use a purchased grid or create your own; it should include a place for student names and boxes for recording progress and mastery. Stickers can be purchased to place in boxes as skills are mastered or homework is completed.

Student Space

- Track students' progress and mastery in areas such as the following:
  - Mastering a skill or set of skills
  - Math facts
  - Reading a certain number of books
  - Reading fluency
- Possible themes for charts and posters include the following:
  - **Race track**—Create a racetrack with a finish line and a race car for each student. Along the racetrack, post "mileposts" that show which skills students are trying to master (multiplication facts, fractions, geometric shapes) or goals they are trying to achieve (number of pages read, number of books read). As students demonstrate mastery or reach a given goal, their race car moves along the racetrack. Once their race car gets to the finish line, the student wins a prize (for example, math flash cards, a new book).
  - **Roller coaster**—Create a roller coaster for which each student has a roller coaster car. Students complete the up-and-down course by mastery of specific skills.
  - **Climbing a mountain**—Create a mountain with mountain climber cut-outs for the students. Students reach the peak by mastering specific skills.
  - **Travel the world**—Using a world map, represent individual skills to be mastered by different countries on the map. Students take a trip around the world by mastering specific skills.
  - **Ice cream sundae**—Using components of an ice cream sundae (for example, scoops of ice cream, whipped cream, cherries, and chocolate sauce) to represent skills to be mastered, students work to build an ice cream sundae until they have an entire sundae completed—and an entire set of skills mastered. Skills could be multiplication tables, with the first scoop representing the twos table, the second scoop representing the threes table, and so on. Once all of the students have completed their ice cream sundaes, the class earns an ice cream party.
  - Suggestions for other "building" charts include building a pizza, with toppings representing skills; building a hamburger, with condiments representing skills.
- For "building" activities, display the items as they are being built, so that students can see exactly where they stand in relation to the goal.

Classroom Learning Centers

Classroom learning centers are an important part of independent exploration and learning. These learning centers are designated areas, usually at a desk or small table, where structured activities are available to students at specific times or when they have finished their work early. Well-organized and well-run learning centers can be a real asset to the classroom.

CONSIDERATIONS

- Establish rules for classroom learning centers.
- Always introduce a new learning center to the class.
- Start with one learning center, and gradually add more centers as you are comfortable introducing them to the class.
- Establish a rotation pattern with a time limit for classroom learning centers. Students move from one center to another to give everyone a turn.
- Set up learning centers to support your themes or units, or simply as an opportunity for free play and exploration. They do not have to be complex or involved.
- Allow students who finish their work early to go to their favorite learning center.
- Use a file folder to create a portable learning center. The activity and its rules can be glued to a folder and laminated, then folded shut. Store the folder in a file box, and any materials can be stored in a plastic zipper bag attached to the folder. To use the portable learning center, a student unfolds it and works at his or her desk.
- Options for classroom learning centers include the following:
  - A designated area in the room
  - An organized station on a desktop

Math Center

- Counting
- Sorting
- Weight (materials: scale, weights or other objects)
- Measurement (materials: ruler, string)
- Measurement (volume)
- Story problems
- Flash cards
- Tangrams
- Practicing fact sheets
- Practicing with timers
- Calculators
- Problem of the day

Science Center

- Growing beans in baggies
- Magnifying glass (observations)
- Electricity (materials: battery, light bulb)
- Magnets
- Animal models
- Simple machines
- Life cycle
- Sink or float
- Reactions (simple)
- Classroom pet (get approval first)

Publishing Center

CONSIDERATIONS

- Write about a picture from a magazine or calendar.
- Create a mini book.
- Create a comic strip.
- Finish a story starter.
- Create a bound book.
- Write a poem.
- Write a letter, such as a letter to a friend, a fictional character, or a historical figure.
- Create a greeting card.
- Write a story on a theme template.
- Write directions or instructions to a prompt.

Clay Table

- Cover the desk with tag paper or butcher paper, and tape down the edges.
- Keep the desk away from windows (because of the effects of the sun).
- Be careful not to mix clay colors together.
- Make sure that students wash their hands before and after using the clay table.
- Encourage students to work with clay as a way of increasing dexterity and developing fine motor skills.

Rug Center

- Board games
- Building sets
- Puzzles
- Teacher's station
- Dress-up
- Animal figures
- Blocks
- Dollhouse
- Electronic games
- Marbles
- Jacks

Listening Center

- Tapes, CDs
- Books on tape, books on CD
- Student readings recorded for playback

Painting Center

CONSIDERATIONS

- Cover the floor under the easel with butcher paper, and secure it with tape.
- Have smocks available for students to place over their clothes.
- Use paint containers with lids to avoid having the paint dry out.
- Establish procedures, especially for clean-up.
- Have students paint a picture of something related to current learning.

Art Center

- Establish rules for use of each art medium, such as paint, clay, pastels, or charcoal.
- Introduce a new art medium several times before you use it in the art center.
- Save paper scraps for the center.
- Keep paper towels, wet wipes, and other clean-up supplies handy.
- Allow students to explore and create freely unless they are being asked to create something related to the current unit of study (for example, a state flag, parts of a plant).

Procedures for Use of Classroom Learning Centers

CONSIDERATIONS

- Establish an order for use of the classroom learning centers.
- Rotate the whole class through each learning center, using a system such as one of the following:
  - Allow students to sign in, entering the date of their turn. Designate a student monitor to maintain the class rotation through the learning centers.
  - Use a clothespin list to track who has used the learning center and who has not. List students' names on a poster and place a clothespin by each name. As students complete their turn, they remove the clothespin by their name and let the next student on the list know to continue the rotation. Once all clothespins have been removed, they can be reattached to begin a new rotation.

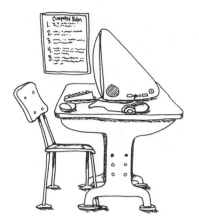

Computer Center

A computer center should be a part of every twenty-first–century classroom. Today's students are tech savvy, and they use technology so much in their day-to-day lives that it has become an essential part of their learning.

CONSIDERATIONS

- Review your school's policies on computer usage and maintenance.
- Incorporate computers into your classroom.
- Place computers near power outlets and an Internet connection.
- Place computers strategically for minimal distraction to other students.
- Allow students to assist you, and you will learn together. Don't waste time feeling inadequate.
- Use headsets for audio components. Headsets are often inexpensive, and using them helps eliminate distractions for other students.
- Train students to use both the computers and the software that you will be using.
- Introduce a computer activity to one student, who in turn can teach another student, and so on.
- Review specific websites that the students are allowed to use with the class. Districts normally have a firewall in place to block potentially inappropriate sites.
- Bookmark favorite sites and show your students how to access them.
- Monitor the software applications. You can set up the computers on a daily basis yourself, or you can arrange for a student monitor to do this.
- Set up folders for each student on the classroom computers. Each student folder can be in a class or subject folder. Show students how to save items in their folders.

17
Computer User
Name and
Password Log

16
Computer
Sign-In Sheet

- Assign student user names and passwords. Use a simple system, and record them in case you need them in the future.
- Create a computer sign-in sheet. This provides a means for the students to use the computer center in an orderly fashion.
- Establish standard procedures for the classroom computer center, which could include the following:
  - Interval rotations—Establish standard intervals every day (20 minutes suggested) when students rotate in and out of the center, usually with a specific program and activity.
  - Early finisher option—Students who finish their work early (and who meet a specific standard of quality for the work) can have time at a classroom computer.
  - Free-time activity
  - One day a week for a specific amount of time
- Sources of classroom computers include the following:
  - School computers assigned to rooms
  - Used computers purchased on eBay, craigslist, or other online source where prices are low (Caution: Be very selective.)
- Sources of funding for classroom computers include the following:
  - Technology grants
  - PTA or Parent Booster Club contributions
  - Donations from local businesses (check district or school policy for such donations)
- Options for student projects using the classroom computer center include the following (suggested software programs appear in parentheses):
  - Research
  - Creating documents and reports (Word, Pages)
  - Creating charts and graphs (Excel, Numbers)
  - Creating movies (iMovie, Final Cut Pro)
  - Creating songs (Garage Band)
  - Creating a web page (iWeb)
  - Creating presentations (PowerPoint, Keynote)
  - Editing and printing photographs (iPhoto)
  - Creating slideshows (PhotoStory, Pro Show Gold, iPhoto)
  - Playing interactive educational games
  - Posting information to a web page, blog, or other interactive site
  - Blogging
  - Visiting museums through video tours
  - Conferencing with other schools and classrooms

Computer Center Rules of Behavior

A good set of rules of behavior for students to follow while using the computer center gives students clear expectations and helps your computer center run smoothly.

CONSIDERATIONS

- Discuss the following with the whole class:
  - Importance of the computer center
  - Hardware (physical components)
  - Software (programs)
  - Computer usage
- Rules of behavior for your classroom computer center could include any of the following (3 to 5 rules suggested):
  - Treat hardware and software with respect and care.
  - Use the computer center only for designated activities.
  - Log on using your own user name and password.
  - Keep your user name and password private.
  - Do not eat or drink near the computers.
  - Store documents in folders as directed by the teacher.
  - Use only your designated file(s).
  - Ask before using a CD, DVD, or flash drive.
  - Use only specified "safe surf" search engines.
  - Do not check e-mail or visit personal websites such as MySpace and Facebook.
  - Use teacher-bookmarked files.
  - Take turns, and work together cooperatively.
  - Ask for assistance if you need it.
  - Do not install any programs.
  - Report any issues with the computer.
  - Respect the time limit.
  - Clean up the computer area when finished.
  - When you are finished, log off and leave the area ready for the next person.
  - Never disconnect equipment.
  - Never insert foreign objects into the computer or peripherals.
  - Never change the monitor settings or desktop.
- Consequences for breaking computer center rules of behavior could include the following:
  - Loss of computer time
  - Loss of recess
  - Note or phone call home

Useful Student and Teacher Websites

Educational websites have much to offer you and your students—educational games, video clips, lesson ideas, and help with computer hardware and software issues.

CONSIDERATIONS

- Before you present a website to your students, visit and use it yourself.
- Check with the district for approved websites.
- Suggested websites include the following:
  - abcya.com—free educational computer games and activities for elementary students
  - bbc.co.uk/schools/typing—an introduction to touch typing for children 7 to 11 years old
  - coolmath4kids.com—fun math-related activities
  - coolmath-games.com—math games and puzzles
  - funbrain.com—fun activities in math and reading
  - geography.learnhub.com/lesson/9828-animaniacs-us-states-and-capitals-song—a fun way to learn geography, including the states and capitals
  - icdlbooks.org—a collection of books representing outstanding historical and contemporary books from throughout the world
  - okaloosa.k12.fl.us/mary/Websites.htm—fun learning tools for elementary school–age children and their families that cover a variety of skills, including reading, memory games, health, math, and problem-solving
  - pbskids.org—games, videos, coloring pages, and other fun activities for kids
  - professorgarfield.com—puzzles, games, and activities in reading, math, art, and music
  - starfall.com—activities that make the classroom more fun for reading and writing, primarily designed for first grade
  - thatquiz.org—self-testing activities in math, science, vocabulary, and geography
  - tumblebooks.com—an interactive reading website including games, puzzles, and quizzes that accompany stories

Conflict Resolution Skills for Students

Students will inevitably have conflicts with one another from time to time, and it is important for them to have appropriate skills for resolving conflicts and problems on their own.

CONSIDERATIONS

- Introduce conflict resolution skills to the students and incorporate practicing them into your classroom.
- Realize that for some students, this is their only exposure to properly resolving a conflict.
- Help students see personal value in properly resolving a conflict. (How does it benefit me? How does it make my life easier?)
- Provide your students with the ability to solve their problems so that they can build confidence and establish positive relationships with others.
- Show students that there are systematic ways of resolving conflicts on their own, allowing them to request the help of an adult only when necessary.
- Remember that many of these conflicts occur during recess, at lunch, after school, or on the bus.
- Allow students to express their frustrations and feelings after they have resolved a conflict, at an appropriate time.
- Review your conflict resolution strategies often.
- Post steps for conflict resolution in your classroom. Refer to them and review them often.
- Practice through role-play.
- Discuss the consequences of different behaviors. Help students understand that resolution is the easiest solution.
- Use conflict resolution slips.

21
Conflict
Resolution Slip
47
Incident
Behavior Log

Student Space

Process

Establish a systematic and easy-to-follow approach to conflict resolution for your students. Review this approach with them several times until they are comfortable following through with it. The approach may include the following steps:

- **Remain calm, don't react.** Take a couple of deep breaths, then count to 10.
- **Step back and assess.** Ask yourself what is happening, and if it is really a big deal. If not, let it go and walk away.
- **Talk, compromise, resolve.** If the situation is important, and walking away won't solve the problem, talk to the other person calmly about what has happened. See if the two of you can come up with a compromise or a solution.
- **Seek peer assistance.** If working directly with the other person doesn't result in a compromise or solution, seek out a respected peer or an older student who can help the two of you discuss the problem and resolve it.
- **Seek an adult's help.** If none of these steps works for you, find an adult to help resolve the problem—but explore all other alternatives first.

Practice

In order for students to successfully resolve a conflict without adult intervention, they must practice the skills that they will need when a conflict arises.

CONSIDERATIONS

- Use a variety of activities to help your students practice conflict resolution skills:
  - Role-play
  - Writing prompts
  - Creating plays for younger students
  - Comic strips
- Develop scenarios to use in practicing conflict resolution skills with your students. Suggestions for scenarios include the following:
  - A classmate yells, "That's my ball! Drop it now!" as you pick up a ball that has been kicked in your direction, interrupting your hopscotch game. All you were going to do is return the ball so you could finish your own game, but now you are angry for being yelled at for nothing.
  - During art class, the teacher says that there are not enough paintbrushes and that pairs of students have to share. You and your partner have to choose who goes first, but you already have your poster idea ready to go and you have been waiting all week for art class.
  - On the playground before school starts, you accidentally step on a classmate's foot. The classmate gets angry and yells, "I'm going to beat you up after school!"

- You have forgotten to bring your completed homework to school, even though it's finished and sitting on your desk at home. It's recess, and you want to go outside to play, but your teacher says you have to go to recess detention, because you didn't bring your assignments to school. You are given a hall pass to walk to detention, but you are frustrated, because *you* know you did your work on time.
- During math class, you get permission to get up to throw a piece of paper in the trash. When you return to your desk, you find that a classmate has taken your pen and won't give it back.

Beyond the Classroom: Field Trips

Field trips are excellent learning opportunities for students, taking learning far beyond the classroom.

CONSIDERATIONS

* Relevant
* Academic-related (supporting grade-level standards)
* Enjoyable
* Student-friendly and accessible

Prior to Field Trip Day

CONSIDERATIONS

* Be prepared.
* Obtain a district-approved list of appropriate grade-level–specific field trips.
* Check the school calendar and obtain your school principal's approval.
* Discuss the field trip with other grade-level teachers. If possible, plan the trip with another class or possibly with several classes. Sometimes group rates apply.
* Complete all necessary paperwork for your school, your district, and the field trip site.
    * School—administrative approval, cafeteria lunch orders
    * District—official permission slip (emergency contact and/or release)
    * Field trip site—date and time, available tours, extra activities that require a reservation

24
Field Trip
Checklist

- Visit the field trip site in advance, if possible. If not, call for details or ask another teacher who has already visited the site for information.
  - Travel time
  - Bus parking
  - Admission
  - Conditions
  - Where to eat lunch
  - Restroom locations
  - Nearest hospital
- Invite parent chaperones at least one or two weeks in advance. Arrange for one parent for every 10 students.
- Ask an administrator about the school policy on requesting money for field trip expenses.
- Prepare identification tags for your students. Include the school name and school phone number. Avoid using the students' names, which would allow a stranger to call a student by name.
- Determine partners for the day. Even older students need a partner and need to be responsible for their partner.
- Reconfirm the visit with the field trip site a day or two in advance.
- Prepare or reserve an emergency backpack.
  - First aid kit
  - Emergency contacts
  - Medical forms
  - Disposable blankets
  - A few bottles of water
  - Simple snack
- Prepare your students before the visit.
  - Details on the field trip site
  - Visiting the field trip site's website for additional information
  - Discussing the goals of the visit
  - Reviewing objectives of the field trip
  - Discussion of expectations
  - What to look for (Develop a list, or possibly develop a scavenger hunt specific to the field trip site.)
  - Consequences for inappropriate behavior

Field Trip Day

- Relax and know that everything will be fine.
- Remind the office that your class will be away for the field trip during the school day.
- Take a student head count, and leave the names of any absent students in the office.
- Confirm all arrangements with the chaperones, give them an overview of the day, and exchange cell phone numbers.
- Chaperone duty could include the following:
  - Assisting with an assigned group of students
  - Notifying you of any behavior problems
  - Staying with their assigned students at all times
  - Sticking to the schedule
  - Confirming bus arrival
  - Distributing identification tags
  - Assigning partners
  - Assisting with restroom trips
  - Collecting lunches and making sure that the lunches are on the bus
  - Being in charge of the emergency backpack
  - Leaving signed releases in the office
  - Carrying emergency contact information
  - Discussing bus procedures with the driver
  - Making sure that proper bus procedures are followed
  - Confirming lunchtime
  - Assisting with lunch on location
  - Confirming departure times

25
Field Trip
Roster

At the Field Trip Site

- Notify personnel at the field trip site of your arrival and meet with your contact person.
- Line students up with their partners and assign chaperones to student groups.
- Follow site procedures for the trip.
- Follow the lunch plan.
- Depart at your scheduled time.

Follow-Up

- Thank all of the volunteer chaperones.
- Write thank-you letters to the field trip site or write personal e-mails as a thank-you.
- Review the field trip day with the students and talk about what they learned.
- Follow-up activities could include the following:
  - Stories
  - Reports
  - Researching aspects of interest
  - Photo collage of the field trip
  - Movie of the field trip
  - Activity sheets that support and relate to the field trip

Sources for Field Trip Funding

Funding might be limited. However, most schools have budget allocations every year for one or two field trips per classroom or grade level.

Funding for field trips could potentially be received from any or all of the following sources:

- School or district
- PTA
- Parent booster club
- Local businesses
- Fee waiver from the field trip site
- Grants

WEST
Student and Teacher Space

The West side of the room is where small group instruction takes place. Student work is easily accessible in this area, a place where students are motivated, rewarded, and incorporated into the learning process. Because the West side of the room is key to the classroom running smoothly and successfully, keeping this area clean, organized, and functional is important.

This section leads you through some simple ways to set up space for small group instruction, including tips for helping students organize their own possessions. We help you manage your classroom by providing ways to support students who are struggling. Included, too, are some easy-to-use strategies for designing and organizing student portfolios for writing, math, science, social studies, and art.

We list some motivators to help maintain student engagement, together with incentives and rewards that keep your students eager to come to school each day. For those 5 to 10 minutes of downtime (for example, before recess, lunch, or the end of the school day) when you need an idea for a quick academic-related activity to keep students engaged, we provide some filler ideas for you to use.

Look for help with the following:

✓ Organizing the Closet and Sink Areas *page 116*
✓ Small Group Instruction *page 119*
✓ Intervention and Support for the Struggling
   Student *page 122*
✓ Student Portfolios *page 126*
✓ Motivators and Incentives *page 130*
✓ Classroom Fillers *page 140*

Organizing the Closet and Sink Areas

Organization in your classroom is essential to doing a good job, being efficient with your time, and making a good impression. Well-organized closet and sink areas play a significant role in letting your students see that keeping things clean and organized is important. When you are organized and orderly, so are your students.

Closet

CONSIDERATIONS

- Start out with a well-organized closet the very first week of school, and make it a habit to keep it that way.
- Give students a sense of responsibility for their personal property and space by modeling good organization.
- Orient students to keeping the closet neat and orderly, including the following:
  - Where and how to hang up their backpacks and jackets
  - Where supplies are kept
  - How supplies are stored
- Keep the closet clutter-free. Backpacks can be hung up.
- Consider organizing instructional materials by curricular areas for easy access.
- Keep all books neat, orderly, and on an easily accessible shelf.
- Place regularly used items in the middle of the closet for easy access.
- Store heavier items on lower shelves.
- Store large boxes at the bottom of the closet for easy access.
- Make sure that no potentially dangerous items are in a closet accessed by students.

Supplies

Supplies are typically available at the school site, usually by request. Check with the office for request forms and procedures for requesting supplies. Once you have your supplies, organize them neatly in your supply closet.

The following is a list of supplies that you could expect to use in your classroom:

- Paper
  - Copy paper
  - Writing paper
  - Lined paper (grade-appropriate for grades K, 1, 2–3, 4–5)
  - Story paper (grades K–2)
  - Graph paper (math)
  - Newsprint (math scratch paper, drawing)
  - Student journals
  - Word cards
  - Sentence strips
  - Lined tag board
  - Poster board
  - Chipboard
  - Index cards
  - Post-it Notes
- Arts and crafts
  - Heavy drawing paper
  - Watercolor paper
  - 9″ × 12″ construction paper
  - 12″ × 18″ construction paper
  - Tissue paper
  - Butcher paper
  - Yarn
  - Cord
  - Brad fasteners
  - Glue bottles
  - Glue sticks
  - Rubber cement
  - Liquid starch
  - Paint (water color and/or tempera)
  - Paint cups
  - Paintbrushes
  - Felt
  - Pipe cleaners
  - Clothespins
  - Metal closing rings
  - Clamps and clips

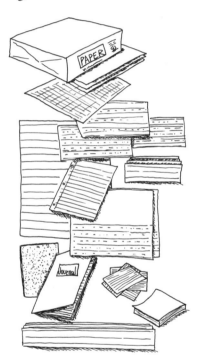

- Markers
- Crayons
- Colored pencils
- Large blue pencils (grades K–2)
- Standard No. 2 pencils (grades 2–5)
- Chalk
- Dry-erase markers
- Erasers
- Scotch tape
- Clear packing tape
- Masking tape
- Bookbinding tape
- Pens
- Overhead markers
- Permanent markers
- File folders
- Stapler
- Staples
- Staple remover
- Paper clips
- Sticky putty
- Student scissors
- Teacher scissors

Sink

CONSIDERATIONS

- Keep the sink area clean and organized.
- Make sure that soap and paper towels are always available at the sink.
- Check with the school for a list of district-approved cleaning products.
- Clean the sink area once a week to kill germs. Use an approved cleanser.
- Store lunch containers (and snacks that could leak) on the ledge of the sink for easy clean-up.
- Art supplies that involve clean-up with water can be stored at the sink, including the following:
  - Paintbrushes, paint cups, and trays
  - Printing rollers
  - Tempera paints
  - Liquid starch

Small Group Instruction

Cooperative learning that involves small groups of two or more students can be very powerful and useful for all three types of learners—auditory, visual, and kinesthetic. Part of the success of small group instruction is productive grouping—organizing the groups in such a way that their potential for success is maximized.

30
Group
Organizer

Suggested Structures for Small Groups

Student Teams

- Teams of students work together to review a lesson.
- Students are placed in groups of four.
- Heterogeneous teams—girls and boys, students of different cultures, high- to low-achieving students, and students of varying abilities—all work well and are designed to include everyone.
- All students take responsibility for helping one another learn.
- A quiz or tangible outcome offers motivation and demonstrates what they have learned.

31
Group Rotation
Planner

The Jigsaw

- The teacher proposes a topic and breaks it down into subtopics.
- Students are placed in groups of six, called "home teams."
- Each "home team" is responsible for learning about a specific subtopic.
- Students work in their groups to master the subtopic.
- Each "home team" shares what has been learned among its group members, and then shares it with the rest of the class.
- This builds comprehensive knowledge of a topic.

Think-Pair-Share

- The teacher poses a relevant question.
- Students *think* about the question.
- Students *pair* up to discuss possible answers to the question.
- Each pair will then *share* their answers with the whole class.
- Think-pair-share works well with most subject areas.

Small Group Guidelines

Small group instruction is most productive when you develop guidelines that help organize student learning and sharing out. Suggested guidelines include the following:

- Each student has a role in the final product of that group.
- All students are accountable for their work in the group.
- Students support one another and develop a relationship based on trust.
- Students communicate well with one another.
- Students in small groups follow a reasonable timeline for completing their tasks.
- All students understand the well-defined goals and the clear expectations for student outcomes.

Small Group Roles

Assigning each student a specific role or responsibility in the group ensures that all students participate. Because each of these roles is important, the group functions well only when every student performs well in his or her assigned role. As groups are formed for different classroom assignments, the roles should be rotated so that each student has the chance to experience the responsibilities of every role.

These roles might include, but are not limited to, the following:

- The **resource** retrieves materials for the group.
- The **recorder** writes down data or information as the group talks.
- The **timer** keeps track of time and makes sure that the group is able to stay on task in order to meet the deadline.
- The **facilitator** makes sure that all students in the group are participating and focusing on their roles. The facilitator also helps keep the discussion on track.
- The **advice consultant** asks the teacher questions related to the task that the group cannot answer for themselves.
- The **reporter** shares the data or information gathered by the group back to the class.

Rotation of Groups

Dividing the class into learning groups that rotate to different activities gives you an opportunity to meet with each group and focus on specific skills with a small group of students.

CONSIDERATIONS

- Rotate all groups daily or on designated days.
- Divide students into three groups for a rotation of teacher, independent, and aide/volunteer groups.
- Meet with a small group to review the daily lesson and/or standard.
- Practice rotations with the whole class prior to rotating.
- List the students in each group. Use index cards or sticky notes for students' names, because groups may change.
- Name each group for easy reference, such as using colors for group names (for example, the "red group").
- Use a timer to signal to the whole class that it's time to switch groups.

30
Group Organizer

31
Group Rotation Planner

Teacher Group (20 minutes)

- Review of lesson
- Informal assessment of skills
- Dictation
- Modeling skills, such as writing or math

Independent Group (20 minutes)

- Writing
- Follow-up activities
- Skill practice
- Illustrating
- Summarizing

Aide/Volunteer Group (20 minutes)

- Reading
- Flashcards
- Educational games
- Building words

Rules for Group Rotation

- Unless there is an emergency, do not interrupt the teacher's group.
- Finish all the "must do" activities and then move on to the "may do" activities.
- Keep the noise level to a minimum.

Intervention and Support for the Struggling Student

A struggling student with learning or behavioral issues can be challenging—even overwhelming at times. Knowing how to support such a student not only helps you provide the modifications needed for the student, but also helps you manage your classroom.

Learning Modifications

Learning modifications are specific strategies that can be used to support the struggling student. Sometimes all that is needed is a modification of the way the material is presented. We provide several of these strategies below.

Scaffolding

Build a lesson on prior knowledge.

- Start with fundamental skills.
- Slowly build on skills.

Preteach/Reteach

Give struggling students additional help both before and after teaching the lesson to the whole class.

- Teach the main points of a lesson to struggling students before teaching it to the whole class (preteach).
- Teach the full lesson to the whole class.
- Summarize the main points of the lesson for struggling students after the full lesson has been taught (reteach).

Proximity

- Seat students who are struggling closer to the front of the room.
- Seat students who are struggling closer to the teacher.

Front-Loading

Build a knowledge base for struggling students before teaching the lesson.

* Review material such as vocabulary, facts, and concepts with struggling students.
* Teach the lesson.

One-on-One

Provide individual assistance to struggling students.

* Work with a student individually.
* Address the specific needs of that student and offer encouragement tailored to the student's efforts.

Chunking

* Divide information into "chunks" (main ideas).
* Teach "chunks" of information to struggling students in separate, shorter lessons.

Learning Styles

Each student is unique in the way he or she learns. Understanding how each student learns best and providing for each learning style are important. Below are some suggested methods for teaching to each of the different learning styles.

Auditory

An auditory learner learns best by hearing information.

* Creating raps
* Read-alouds
* Presenting
* Whole class discussion
* Singing

Visual

A visual learner learns best by seeing information.

* Posters and charts
* Movies and DVDs
* Demonstrations
* Photos
* iMovie projects
* PowerPoint presentations

Kinesthetic

A kinesthetic learner learns best through hands-on experiences.

- Constructing models
- Role-play
- Drawing
- Dance

Subject Interventions

It is helpful to have some specific tools and strategies to use in the different subject areas of your curriculum for students who are struggling.

Math

- Flash cards for math facts
- Manipulatives
- Computer games

Language Arts

- Reading to students
- Sight word practice
- Writing comic strips and/or story boards
- Phonics, blending, and decoding
- Word building with letter cards
- Fluency practice by timed reading
- Dictation

Difficult Behavior

09
Behavior
Tracker

Students demonstrate difficult behavior when they act out and are disruptive in class.

CONSIDERATIONS

- Build on a student's strength.
- Find something good about a disruptive student—anything—that you can build on.
- Don't take the difficult behavior of a student personally.
- Take small steps.

Distraction

Sometimes a student's behavior can be managed by providing a diversion or distraction from the disruptive behavior.

- Give the student a Koosh ball to hold and manipulate.
- Give the student a straw to chew on.

Relationship

If you build a stronger relationship with a disruptive student, that student may well be more responsive to you in teaching situations.

• Talk to the student and spend some time getting to know the student better.
• Give the student responsibility.

Contract

A contract is an agreement between the teacher and the student that monitors student behavior and specifies consequences (both positive and negative) for specific behaviors.

• Write up a contract specific to a struggling student's behavior—both the problem behavior and the behavior desired.
• Monitor behavior.
• Follow through with the agreed-upon consequences for actual behavior.

Creative Projects

Hands-on, design-oriented projects are often very effective with struggling students.

• Creative projects keep students engaged.
• All students have an equal opportunity to succeed.

Signal

When a teacher gives a specific signal to a struggling student, it serves to remind the student that the current behavior is disruptive and should be changed.

• Establish a signal to give when disruptive behavior is escalating.
• Suggested signals are a particular facial expression, rubbing the back of your head, or a tap on the table.

Student Portfolios

Student portfolios are where the students' best work is kept. The portfolios are continually upgraded as students improve their skills and add improved work samples. They are not work folders; rather, they are collections of highlighted work.

CONSIDERATIONS

- Portfolios can be a collective body of work that either spans the curriculum or is broken down by subject area.
- Students take part in choosing which work they want to showcase in their student portfolios.
- Comments can be posted on each piece of work to explain why the student chose that particular piece to include in the portfolio.
- There can be up to ten pieces of a student's work in each subject-related folder. However, because it is often a good exercise for students to choose which piece to retire from the folder when adding a new and improved sample of work, you may want to limit each student to fewer samples (for example, three) kept in each portfolio folder.
- Students can share their work with their parents during teacher-parent-student conferences, explaining their work, for a much more powerful and meaningful conference.

Portfolio Tips

Maintenance of portfolios can be handled without much teacher oversight once students are taught how to manage them. Teaching students how to maintain their own portfolios encourages them to take their work seriously and show pride in the pieces they want to showcase.

- Select the subject areas for your students' portfolios. Writing, math, science, social studies, and art, for example, are all appropriate for student portfolios.
- Create folders or boxes where student portfolios can be kept.
- Include assessments in the portfolios, unless you have decided to create assessment boxes in addition to student portfolios.
- Teach students how to review the portfolios as a whole, to make necessary changes on a regular basis, to determine which items to add, and to determine which items should be removed.
- Ask students to get teacher approval, if possible, before adding to a portfolio, so that the student can explain why he or she wants to add that item.
- Decide on a specific number of items to be kept in a student portfolio. Students can then be responsible for maintaining it, removing old items and adding new ones. This keeps a collection of their best work current.

Portfolio Materials

- File folders—convenient to use and easy to store
- Folded tag board or poster board—the student's name can be written on the longer edge
- Cereal box or shoe box
- Outside of the folder or box decorated by students
- Self-portrait of the student at four times during the year on the outside of the portfolio, with each self-portrait dated (This shows evolution in artistic abilities.)

Writing Portfolio

A selection of the student's best writing samples is maintained in a writing portfolio.

CONSIDERATIONS

- Encourage students to include a variety of district-mandated and teacher assessments that cover several different writing experiences.
  - Narratives
  - Letters
  - Expository writing
  - Persuasive essays
- Align the students' samples to state standards to demonstrate the standards being taught, as well as students' progress toward mastery, and grade them using a rubric.

80
Writing
Portfolio

Math Portfolio

A selection of the student's best work in math, as represented by math projects and assessments, is maintained in a math portfolio.

CONSIDERATIONS

- Encourage students to include a variety of district-mandated and teacher assessments that cover an array of math skills.
  - Story word problems
  - Current assessments
  - Newest skills mastered (for example, the times tables)
  - Warm-up activities
  - Problem of the day
- Align the students' samples to state standards to demonstrate the standards being taught, as well as students' progress toward mastery.

Science Portfolio

A selection of the student's best work in science, as represented by science experiments and projects, is maintained in a science portfolio.

CONSIDERATIONS

- Encourage students to include a variety of district-mandated and teacher assessments that cover several different science skills.
  - Investigations
  - Quizzes and tests
  - Pictures of students working in cooperative groups
  - Photos from science-related field trips
- Align the students' samples to your state standards to demonstrate the standards being taught, as well as students' progress toward mastery.

Social Studies Portfolio

A selection of the student's best work in social studies is maintained in a social studies portfolio.

CONSIDERATIONS

- Encourage students to include a variety of district-mandated and teacher assessments that cover several different social studies skills.
  - Illustrated maps
  - Letters to historical figures
  - Quizzes and tests
  - Vocabulary illustrations
  - Related art activities

66
Subject
Portfolio

- Historical reports
- Research projects
- Align the students' samples to your state standards to demonstrate the standards being taught, as well as students' progress toward mastery.

Art Portfolio

A selection of the student's best artwork is maintained in an art portfolio.

CONSIDERATIONS

- Encourage students to include a variety of samples that cover the broad range of artistic work created.
  - Work from an assigned art lesson
  - Illustrations related to other content areas
  - Illustrations unrelated to other content areas
  - Video of a performance
  - Photographs of larger pieces
- Align the students' samples to your state standards to demonstrate the standards being taught, as well as students' progress toward mastery.

Motivators and Incentives

Students' enthusiasm for learning, engagement, and participation can be greatly increased through the use of motivators and incentives in the classroom. These help develop their interests so that they look forward to coming to school each day and being involved in classroom activities.

CONSIDERATIONS

- Understand that learning can't be fun 100% of the time, but it should be engaging.
- Create a space that stimulates motivation to learn.
- Design interesting, relevant, hands-on lessons around an appropriate grade-level curriculum.
- Create an environment where students can be successful.
- Help students understand the value of what they are learning, so that they participate more in the process and therefore comprehend more.

Student Motivation Through Instruction

Increasing the students' desire and interest in their own education is the key to their being motivated. Several proven motivational techniques are provided below.

CONSIDERATIONS

- Realize that the ultimate goal is to develop self-motivated students.
- Remember that incentives can be simple. They don't even have to be purchased. The key is recognition, follow-through, and consistency.
- Realize that all students can benefit from motivators and incentives.

- Let students know that you like them and that you expect good behavior from them.
- Strive to find something good and worthwhile in every student. Every student deserves recognition.
- Play a key role in generating self-confidence and motivation in your students.

Provide Detailed Feedback

Provide students with feedback on all of their submitted work: Students want to know if they have completed their work correctly.

CONSIDERATIONS

- Never give an assignment that you are not willing to score or grade.
- Provide meaningful comments.
- Return students' work with feedback: Unreturned or ungraded work provides no motivation.

Provide Support to Unenthusiastic Students

Students who don't seem to care about schoolwork need extra attention. These are students who struggle, for whom school is a constant challenge just to keep up, and who are often unenthusiastic about learning because of outside factors.

CONSIDERATIONS

- Hold high expectations for *all* students.
- Reinforce students' perceptions of themselves as successful.
- Design instruction that is interesting, relevant, and hands-on.
- Provide opportunities for all students to succeed. You can do this by adding a variety of components—either required or optional—to a lesson: an art component, an oral presentation, or a hands-on project.

Explain the Value of Assigned Tasks

Students are more able to see the value of an assigned task when they know that the lesson has a connection to their own lives.

CONSIDERATIONS

- Relate lessons to the students' own lives.
- Create culturally relevant lessons.
- Create lessons that you know will interest the students.
- Create lessons that require participation by all of the students.
- Keep the students busy, moving, and having fun.

Provide Opportunities for Choice

Students will be more invested in their own success when they have an opportunity to make choices. Allow students to choose from a variety of learning experiences.

CONSIDERATIONS

- Give students a sense of power and ownership in their education.
- Connect learning activities to the individual student's personal interests.
- Provide opportunities for students to choose from a selection of different but equally valuable options.
- Encourage students to finish less attractive assignments by letting them know that they will be able to move on to assignments that they enjoy more.
- Try "must do" and "may do" activities: Students complete "must do" tasks (such as finishing a book report, completing vocabulary sentences, or researching maps) before moving on to "may do" tasks (such as silent reading, working on the computer, or practicing multiplication flashcards).

Show Enthusiasm for What You Are Teaching

Be excited about what you are presenting—your students will pick up on this!

CONSIDERATIONS

- Show your excitement about what you are planning and teaching.
- Plan activities that motivate you and that you are excited about. Students are sensitive to your energy level.
- Act as if you are interested in the subject at hand, even if it isn't your favorite. Fake it if you have to!
- Encourage student participation as much as you can.

Provide Multiple Learning Opportunities

Because students have different learning styles, prepare lessons that have options for students to explore.

CONSIDERATIONS

- Plan two or three different follow-up activities for each lesson.
- Allow students to choose the activity that most appeals to them and their strengths (for example, students are to write an expository essay, but they are allowed to choose the topic).
- Incorporate art, if possible, to give ELL (English language learner) and struggling students an opportunity to demonstrate their learning in ways that don't require words.

Be Creative

Take a novel approach to teaching—try new techniques and applications.

CONSIDERATIONS

- Incorporate a variety of games and other non-standard demonstrations of understanding into your teaching.
- Use different outcomes to measure your students' understanding of projects and presentations.
- Incorporate games like Wheel of Fortune and Jeopardy as innovative ways to assess learning.
- Use fractions in cooking as an innovative way to measure learning.

Incorporate Design

Asking students to work with a project through design and presentation opens an entirely new way of working with content to them.

CONSIDERATIONS

- Give students a specific audience and criteria list for a given project: Who will be reading this? Is it appealing? Is it a good design? Is it clear, concise, and comprehensive?
- Turn a standard project into one of design by shifting the expectations of the students.
- Ask students to design a variety of items, including (but not limited to) travel brochures, advertisements, flyers from supermarkets, mini books, and posters.

Incentives and Rewards

Motivating both individual students and the class as a whole can keep your students on task, excited about learning, and orderly.

CONSIDERATIONS

- Use rewards to help motivate students to complete tasks.
- Consider your reward system carefully. It is a commitment, and you need to be prepared to follow through.
- Encourage students to behave appropriately or to complete work for its own sake. The goal is for your students to do the right thing and feel accomplished because of intrinsic—not extrinsic—factors.
- Don't set up a situation where students feel controlled and manipulated.

- Follow through with any promise of a reward, no matter what it is. If you don't follow through, your students may not trust your future incentive and reward programs.
- Never take a reward back—once it is earned, it is theirs.
- Know your class, and give rewards out as needed, but don't give rewards out too freely. Find a good balance for your specific class.
- Be consistent. When you establish a rewards system, follow through when giving rewards for specific behaviors and for tasks completed.

Simple Incentives and Rewards

There are many simple verbal and nonverbal indicators that you can use to show your students that you recognize and appreciate their behavior or achievement, including the following:

- Remarks such as "Good job!" and "Well done!"
- Praise in front of the whole class
- Congratulations
- Smiles
- Free time
- Special activity, such as cooking
- Stickers
- School supplies
- Treats, such as a special healthy snack or a small piece of candy at the end of the day

Incentive and Reward Systems

Table Points

- Have students work together as a group (by table, row, or desk cluster) to earn points for their group.
- Reward the group that has the most points at the end of the week.

Name Cards

- Have all students make name cards to keep on their desks.
- Place stickers or draw a positive mark on the name card when a desired outcome is exhibited.
- Reward each student who earns a certain number of stickers or marks at the end of the week.

Behavior Chart

Design a behavior chart system that works for you. Ask other teachers how they set up their system, and then borrow or modify what they have found to be successful. A sample behavior chart system using colors to represent categories of behavior is described below.

- Prepare a chart with each student's name and a color-coded system of behavior consequences.
- Assign or change color cards according to the behavior exhibited. (Colored clothespins or individual behavior cards can also be used.)
- Designate "bad behavior" color cards that involve specific consequences.
- Encourage students to behave so that "bad behavior" cards are not assigned to them.
- Reward students who keep the color card representing good behavior all week.
- A color-coded system could include the following:
  - Green—on task = good behavior
  - Yellow—first warning = reminder
  - Blue—second warning = time-out
  - Red—third warning = notify parent

Marbles in a Jar

- Have a designated marble jar to keep track of desired behavior by the class.
- Fill the jar slowly with marbles, each marble representing a time when the class demonstrates the desired behavior.
- Reward the class when the marble jar is full.
- Use this system on a smaller scale, with each table having its own small jar or container that is filled in the same manner.

Money

- Set up a reward system where students earn "incentive money" for desired behavior. This is an excellent way to teach students about money.
- Reward students with incentive money in $1, $5, and $10 denominations for desired behavior.
- Assign a specific dollar amount for specific tasks (for example, cleaning up one's desk = $20, helping a friend = $10).
- Allow students to purchase rewards (such as school supplies) with their money at the end of the week.

41
Incentive
Money

Checks

- Set up a reward system where a certain dollar amount is awarded for specific desired behaviors.
- Print blank "incentive checks" to use on reward days. Ask a bank if they will give you blank checkbook registers or print your own check ledger sheets.
- Teach students how to balance a check ledger.
- Write weekly incentive checks to students for the amount that represents the total of their rewards for specific desired behaviors.

40
Incentive
Checks

39
Incentive
Check Ledger

- Allow students to purchase rewards (such as school supplies) with their checks at the end of the week.
- Provide time for all students to balance their check ledgers.

Spelling Out Words

- Set up a reward system where the class works to spell out the name of the reward they are working toward. The class earns letters in the specific word or phrase for desired behaviors.
- Use this system for earning a field trip or a party. For example, the class would earn letters from the phrase "Valentine's Day Party" or "Field Trip to the Natural History Museum" for those rewards.
- Add one letter to the board to spell out the word or phrase that names the reward whenever the class demonstrates good behavior (for example, when the class is caught doing something that they should be doing without having been asked).

Color a Theme-Related Silhouette

- Draw the silhouette of a theme-related item, such as a Christmas tree, a turkey, or a pumpkin.
- Draw several lines within the silhouette to create a mosaic effect.
- Color in a piece of the mosaic when students demonstrate good behavior, or allow students to color the mosaic pieces.
- Use as many different colors as possible.
- Reward students once all the mosaic pieces have been colored in and the silhouette is complete.

Tickets

42–46
Incentive
Tickets

- Establish a reward system where students receive tickets for good behavior or task completion, and they use tickets to purchase rewards or enter a raffle.
- Keep tickets on hand to distribute throughout the day for good behavior or task completion.
- A system for redeeming the reward tickets might include the following:
  - Option 1: Students write their names on the tickets and keep their own tickets in a plastic zipper bag. At the end of the week, students use tickets to "buy" rewards.
  - Option 2: Students write their names on the tickets and place them in a large bucket. At the end of the week, the teacher draws names for rewards.

Suggested Rewards

Rewards teach students that good behavior and hard work pay off. However, they should never replace a student's own self-motivation to do well.

CONSIDERATIONS

- Keep rewards simple. You don't have to spend money—extra free time or lunch with the teacher works fine.
- Plan some rewards for the class as a collective group and others for individual students.
- Consider rewarding other students for good behavior that a particular student did not demonstrate, rather than singling out a student for bad behavior.
- Follow school and/or district policy when it comes to requesting items to use as rewards. For example, requesting rewards from students might be an option, but it must be cleared with your principal first. Other sources for reward items could be friends or local businesses.
- Purchase rewards from inexpensive retail stores (like dollar stores).

Movie Time and/or Popcorn

- Reward the class or a group of students by showing a movie and/or serving popcorn.
- Reward the whole class for the last hour of a school day or for a table group at lunchtime. This is a good end-of-week activity, so consider scheduling it for a Friday.
- Refer to the school's and/or district's approved movie list, and check with the school about the policy for showing videos.
- Use a fun but educational movie, such as one of the 30-minute Magic School Bus videos.
- Ask about the school's food policy before using popcorn or other food as a reward. Consider buying bags of popcorn or making microwavable popcorn in the teacher's lounge.

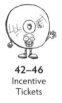

42–46
Incentive
Tickets

Cushions

- Reward students or teams of students with cushions to use for a week.
- Give the student or table group that earns the most points (or gets the most marbles in their jar) a soft chair cushion to sit on for the next week.
- Use cushions that can be tied to chairs.

Gift Cards

- Use purchased gift cards to reward students in a raffle drawing.
- Buy several gift cards from a local bookstore for $5 or $10 each.
- Let students earn tickets that are placed in a jar for the raffle drawing.
- Remind students that the more tickets they earn, the better their chances are.
- Pull out three tickets at the end of the week or month, and present a gift card to the three students whose names are drawn.

Treasure Chest

41
Incentive
Money

42–46
Incentive
Tickets

- Fill a treasure chest with reward items, such as pencils, notebooks, and erasers.
- Option 1: Reward students by allowing them to choose items from the treasure chest on Fridays or at the end of the month.
- Option 2: Reward students by allowing them to purchase items from the treasure chest with "incentive money" or "incentive tickets" on Fridays or at the end of the month.
- Purchase items from websites such as www.orientaltradingcompany.com at low prices.

Computer Center or Learning Center Time

- Reward students with extra time at the computer center or classroom learning centers.
- Use this reward with either the whole class or small groups.
- Allow extra time at the specified center at the end of a school day or on Friday.

Game or Activity

- Reward the whole class with a special game or classroom activity.
- Use points, marbles, or another item to keep track of progress toward the reward.
- Reward the students with an indoor game, an outdoor game, or a special art activity. (This should in no way replace physical education or art. This is extra, not part of the curriculum.)

Lunch with the Teacher

- Reward students by staying with them during the lunch period and enjoying lunch time with them.
- Check with the school about its policy on eating in the classroom. If this is not allowed, eat with the students in the cafeteria and then return to the classroom.

- Allow a specific group of students (such as table groups, rows of students, or students who have a certain number of stickers or positive marks on their name cards by Wednesday) to bring their lunch to the classroom on Friday.
- Have lunch with the students, and then allow them to play board and/or computer games during the rest of the lunch period.
- Be sure you can follow through with this—after all, you are giving up your own lunch time.

Behavior Certificates

- Reward students with behavior certificates for a designated time period (for example, a week or a month) that are sent home for parents to see.
- Purchase or create a handful of fun certificates to send home with students who have earned them.
- Create a simple behavior certificate using an index card with a sticker and the words "Good Citizen" on it.

34–38
Incentive
Certificates

- Present certificates on a consistent basis, and parents will come to expect them.
- Send a certificate home with everyone in the class when the whole class has earned a reward. This is a real boost for students who aren't often acknowledged.

Additional Rewards
(Especially for Those on Behavior Contracts)

- Teacher helper
- Office helper
- Line leader
- Care for the class pet
- Read with a buddy
- Tell the class a joke
- Listen to a taped story
- Help in another classroom
- Read a text selection to the class
- 5- to 10-minute free-choice activity
- Free library period
- Happy note home

Classroom Fillers

Fillers—or sponge activities—use the time between lessons on activities in a fun yet educational way. These short activities absorb the short bits of time that occur throughout the school day. Several suggested classroom fillers are included below.

CONSIDERATIONS

- Keep fillers related to academic work, but fun and simple, too.
- Use fillers when there are only 5 to 15 minutes left in the period or at the end of the day.
- Use fillers for rainy or snowy day schedules, when the students have to stay inside during recess and lunch.

Around the World

Around the World is a whole-class game where students answer questions or give answers for flash cards. They work their way through the group to get "around the world."

- Students stand behind their seats.
- Choose a starting person and the rotation to be used.
- The first student in the rotation stands beside the second student in the rotation at the second student's seat.
- The teacher holds up a flash card.
- The first student of the pair to answer correctly moves to stand beside the next student in the rotation.
- The student who did not answer remains where he or she is.
- This continues until at least one student makes it completely "around the world" (around the entire rotation or class).

- An alternate setup is for students to stand in a circle, and the student who answers correctly moves to stand behind the next student in the rotation.
- This activity works well with vocabulary, math facts, picture cards for foreign language learning, and other content-based material.

Bingo

This is classic bingo with an educational twist.

10, 11
Bingo

- Print a blank bingo card for each student.
- Provide a list of items to be entered on the bingo cards, such as a range of numbers, vocabulary words, or pictures of items.
- List more items than can fit on the cards so that each student's card will be different.
- Students fill out their own cards from the list provided.
- Read the problem or definition out loud.
- Students cover a correct answer with a bingo chip.
- The game continues until someone gets a complete row across, down, or diagonally and can shout out "Bingo!"

SUGGESTION

- Choose items by using a set of flash cards to randomly select math facts, picture cards for vocabulary, lists of spelling words, definition cards for vocabulary, or lists of synonyms and antonyms.

I Spy

Students can play the classic I Spy game in a version that has an educational purpose. There are many variations of this basic game that can be used in the classroom.

- "Spy" an object.
- Say "I spy something _____," where you complete the sentence with a clue to help students guess the object.

SUGGESTIONS

- Use the game to teach colors, shapes, and sizes. For example, "spy" right angles in the classroom after teaching the concept in math.
- Identify items around the classroom when teaching basic vocabulary to ESL (English as a Second Language) students.
- Develop a group of items to be "spied" by having students write down item names or draw pictures of items on small sheets of paper.
- Divide students into teams to play the game as a friendly competition.
- Play the game with a goal in mind, such as cleaning up scraps on the floor after an art project.

Monster Madness

Have students draw creatures using traced letters as the base. This is a great learning activity for the lower grades.

- Have each student choose a letter to use as the base for their creature.
- Allow the students to trace their chosen letter from a stencil or die-cut machine.
- Have students draw a creature, monster, or character out of their chosen letter.

SUGGESTIONS

- Use numbers as well as letters.
- Have this activity available for students to work on throughout the day.
- Establish a learning center with stencils and markers where students can draw their creatures.
- Display the "monsters" on bulletin boards and around the room.
- Allow each student to create an entire family of creatures, using all the letters of his or her name.

Chain Story

Students cooperate with each other to create a chain story, using selected words from lessons.

- Prepare a set of index cards, each of which has one spelling word or vocabulary word written on it.
- Arrange the class in a circle or allow them to work from their seats.
- Hand out the index cards, one to each student.
- Pick a student to start the story. The student will use the word on the index card in his or her part of the story—about one or two sentences.
- Have each student in turn add another sentence or two to the story, using the word on his or her index card.

SUGGESTIONS

- Assign a specific topic for the story, or let the students decide the topic.
- Divide students into groups so that each group creates a story to share with the class.

Twenty Questions

Students ask a series of up to 20 "yes" and "no" questions in an attempt to guess a person, place, or thing related to material currently being studied.

- Pick a topic related to a current area of study.
- Ask one student to think of a person, place, or thing related to that topic. The rest of the class is not told what it is.
- Have the other students try to guess what that something is by asking "yes" and "no" questions.

- The student that picked the person, place, or thing must answer only "yes" or "no" to the questions asked.
- The class can ask a maximum of 20 questions in trying to guess the correct answer.

- Use this activity as a unit opener.

Top Ten

Students develop lists of 10 items in different categories.

- Have the students make lists of the top 10 concepts for a topic you are studying.

- For something less challenging, have students list everyday items, such as their 10 favorite foods, music groups, athletes, or television shows.
- If you have more time, have students alphabetize their lists.

What's in the Bag?

Students try to guess what item is in a bag.

- Choose an item that is related to a story you have been reading, a social studies topic, or a science concept the class has been studying.
- Place the item in a brown bag (or other opaque bag).
- Have the students sit in a circle.
- Carry the bag around the circle, letting students feel the item without looking inside.
- Ask students not to share their ideas out loud until they are asked to do so.
- Give everyone a chance to think about what the item might be.
- Draw 5 to 10 names randomly from a deck of cards or popsicle sticks.
- Let those 5 to 10 students share their guesses, and list their guesses on the board.
- Reveal the item's identity.

- In order to eliminate certain guesses, have students list the characteristics that they were able to determine from touching the item. Narrow the choices down to those that fit the descriptions.
- Use this activity with students in the lower grades to identify fruits and vegetables.
- Use this activity with ELLs (English language learners) to improve their ability to explain physical attributes.

When You Only Have a Few Minutes,
Try These Ideas ...

- List as many objects in the room as you can.
- Give multiplication or division problems, and have students call out answers.
- List the continents of the world.
- Name as many countries, state capitals, cartoon characters, or kinds of natural disasters as you can.
- Find countries on a map.
- Name as many colors as you can that are not one of the colors of the rainbow.
- List as many types of transportation as you can in each of these categories—by air, by land, by sea.
- Write the name of a food that begins with each letter of the alphabet.
- List as many home electronic devices as you can.
- Look at a picture, and use as many nouns, verbs, adverbs, and adjectives as possible to describe it.
- Draw a picture from a description of characteristics and attributes.
- Brainstorm a list of words for a specific theme (for example, autumn, space, heroes, and holidays).

AERIAL VIEW
Looking Down from Above

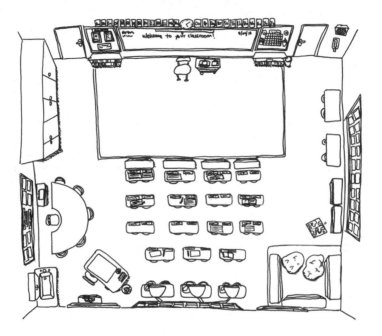

The Aerial View lets you see the big picture—
the setup and management of the classroom for the
school year. After all, how you set up and manage your classroom is critical to maximizing your delivery of instruction.

In this section, you have access to a number of terrific ideas that will be useful
to you when taking a look at your classroom from the top down. A classroom
design that is well organized and allows your classroom to function well creates a
comfortable environment for both you and your students. Everything about how
your students are managed—from their traffic patterns to their homework, from
how they are graded to how they work with the classroom aide—needs to be decided and implemented from day one. As the year progresses and your teaching
and management styles evolve, you can modify and adapt how things are done to
better suit your evolving style and this year's particular group of students.

Look for help with the following:

First Day Reminders

There is nothing like the first day of school, when even veteran teachers get butterflies and wonder if they have forgotten anything. In looking at the big picture, there are a few first day reminders that ought to be considered.

CONSIDERATIONS

- Remember that parents and students are also nervous.
- Be organized—this will help you handle anything that you might have forgotten.
- Ask for help if you need it.

On the First Day of School

CONSIDERATIONS

- Introduce yourself to your students.
  - Consider sharing a little personal information.
  - Share only what you are comfortable with. Start slow. You may want to show your students some pictures of yourself, and perhaps your family or your pets.
- Talk about classroom and school procedures.
  - Keep it simple, with a focus on activities like pencil sharpening, hanging up backpacks, lining up to enter and exit the classroom, and so on.
- Distribute name tags or have students make their own.
  - Have younger students wear their name tags.
  - Have older students display their name tags on their desks.

- Take attendance.
  - Discuss tardiness and absenteeism.
  - Discuss the excuse policy, for example, when students need to bring a written note from a parent.
- Preview the year.
  - Talk to students about upcoming units and some interesting ideas you have for the curriculum this year.
  - Share your enthusiasm! It motivates them for the year.
- Distribute materials.
  - Assign and distribute textbooks and consumables (record these on an inventory sheet).
  - Discuss responsibility and care for materials.
  - Distribute journals for writing, math, and other subjects.
  - Distribute supplies, such as desktop boxes and pens.

70
Textbook
Inventory

- Engage students.
  - Introduce "getting to know you" activities such as an "I Am" or "I Come From" poem (these can be found online).
  - Use this time to circulate and get to know students.
- Take a tour of the school with your class (especially for lower grades).
  - Discuss procedures for going to the restroom, the office, or the nurse.
  - Discuss procedures for leaving the school campus.
  - Explain the policy for hall passes.
- Introduce a writing activity.
  - Try to avoid topics like "My Summer Vacation." Instead, assign a topic with a bit more significance and less superficiality, such as "People I Look Up To," "My Future Career," or "Goals for This School Year." After all, which topic will give you more information about your students?
  - Have younger students draw a picture to go with their writing.
- Establish classroom rules.
  - Have some classroom rules in mind, and guide students to come up with similar ones.
  - Develop classroom rules and consequences as a whole class, with as much participation by the students as possible.
  - Remember that students are more invested when they are included in the process.
  - Have students write down the classroom rules so they can take them home to be signed by their parents.
- Get to know your students.

65
Student Interest
Survey

  - Have students complete a student interest survey to provide you with more personal information about them.

Classroom Design

When you create a classroom environment that is functional and organized, yet comfortable for you and your students to inhabit day in and day out, you lay the groundwork for a good school year. The physical appearance of your classroom is also the first impression people will have of it.

CONSIDERATIONS

- Develop a clear vision of what you want as the physical setup of your classroom this year, so that you can arrange that first.
- Walk yourself through a typical day. Decide where to place the student desks and where to have the common area (for example, placement of a rug) to best facilitate your plans. The placement of these items will affect everything that happens in your classroom.
- Visit other classrooms, and ask for advice from experienced teachers.
- Establish a classroom environment that promotes student involvement, encourages self-control, and minimizes disruptions that are caused by disorganization.
- Make sure that your classroom reflects care and respect for you and your students.

Physical Setup of the Classroom

Setting up your classroom in a systematic way can reduce confusion and make the instructional process easier.

CONSIDERATIONS

- Set up the furniture and rug.
  - Student desks and chairs
  - Teacher's desk and chair
  - File cabinet
  - Bookcases
  - Small group workstation
  - Learning center desks and chairs
- Organize all supplies, having requested them from the office.
  - Teacher supplies at the teacher's desk
  - Student supplies at the student desks or in closets
  - Room supplies in closets
- Organize books and consumables (to be distributed).
- Set up the classroom library.
  - Two or three bookcases or plastic tubs
  - Small rug
  - Beanbag chair
- Set up classroom equipment.
  - CD player
  - Overhead projector
  - Document reader
  - Smart Board
- Set up computers.
  - Power outlet
  - Internet connection
  - Monitor
  - Printer
- Mount bulletin boards.
  - Background paper and borders
  - Calendar
  - School news and information board
- Set up the teacher station near the front of the room.
- Set up workspace for the aide or volunteer.
  - Learning tools
  - Supplies for students
- Set up learning centers.

23
Equipment
Inventory

Purposeful Classroom Arrangement

A room arrangement that lends itself to your teaching style, student movement around the classroom, and facilitation of instruction is of the utmost importance. After all, this is where you and your students spend most of your waking hours.

CONSIDERATIONS

- Organize your classroom so that movement can take place easily and in an orderly fashion.
- Take into account the needs of all persons involved.
- The arrangement of the classroom must meet many needs, including the following:
  - Students working individually
  - Students working in pairs
  - Small group work
  - Students working in centers
  - Multiple types of instruction
  - Equal access to instruction
  - Equipment usage

High-Traffic Areas

There are several areas of the classroom that students move through or use frequently. Special consideration must be given to these high-traffic areas.

CONSIDERATIONS

- Keep high-traffic areas free of clutter.
- Make these areas accessible, planned, and well organized.
- Remember that high-traffic areas become easy targets for misbehavior if they are not carefully monitored.
- Keep high-traffic areas clearly separated to avoid any confusion about where students should be at any given time.
- Set up the desks so that the teacher can reach students easily and move around the room without obstruction.
- Have more than one pencil sharpener and trash can to avoid clustering of students.
- High-traffic areas could include the following:
  - Common area
  - Learning centers
  - Small group instruction area
  - Teacher's workstation
  - Classroom library
  - Pencil sharpener
  - Trash can
  - Recycling bin
  - Coat racks

Floor Space

The floor space in your classroom is limited, and each piece of furniture takes up some of that floor space. You must take into account the footprint of each piece as you decide which arrangement of the several pieces of furniture works best for you and your students.

CONSIDERATIONS

- Walk around your classroom. Note the sizes of the student desks, teacher's desk, tables, carts, bookcases, computer stations, and other large furniture and equipment.
- Draw a few possible arrangements of the furniture. Viewing options on paper helps avoid moving heavy furniture more than is necessary.
- Decide which of these possible arrangements works best for your classroom this year.
- Take care not to block electrical outlets. You may need them in your final classroom design.
- Allow plenty of room for maneuverability for yourself and your students.
- Do not block emergency exits.

Student Desk Arrangement

The need to position students' desks so that all students have equal access to instruction is a primary factor in the physical arrangement of your classroom. Three instructional formats—whole class, small groups, and individuals—are discussed below.

CONSIDERATIONS

- Consider the different kinds of activities your class will be engaged in.
- Visit other classrooms at your grade level, and consider the classroom arrangements there.
- Assign seating, rather than allowing free choice, in order to keep students from sitting next to their friends.
- Implement a seating arrangement that contributes to a heterogeneous classroom.
- Determine what works best for your class this year, given your teaching style.

Whole Class

When you are teaching the entire class at once, the seating arrangement must allow all of the students full access to instruction from a single focal point in the classroom.

- Arrange student desks so that all students face the focal point of the classroom where you will be teaching.
- Typical desk arrangements for the whole class include the following:
  - Rows of small tables or desks
  - Desks arranged in a U shape so that all eyes are directed toward the board

Small Groups

When groups of four or more students work together, the students must be able to interact with each other without being distracted by other activities in the classroom.

CONSIDERATIONS

- Arrange student desks in clusters so that the students in each cluster are facing one another.
- Typical desk arrangements for small groups include the following:
  - Four students—two desks facing each other
  - Six students—two desks facing each other with an additional desk at each end

Individuals

When students are working individually, each student should have personal workspace that minimizes distractions from other students.

CONSIDERATIONS

- Typical desk arrangements that allow for individual workspace are the following:
  - Rows of individual desks
  - Tables placed side by side so that all students are facing the front of the room

Teacher's Desk Area

The placement of the teacher's furniture and equipment affects not only your efficiency during the day, but also the effectiveness of your instructional delivery.

Teacher's Desk

CONSIDERATIONS

- Realize that you will rarely sit at your desk during the school day.
- Store frequently used teaching materials at the teacher's desk.
- Consider placing the teacher's desk nearest the space where whole class instruction takes place so that materials are readily available.

File Cabinets and Personal Storage Cabinets

CONSIDERATIONS

- Consider placing file cabinets and storage cabinets adjacent to the teacher's desk for ready access to supplies, materials, and paperwork.
- Lock cabinets that contain student information in order to maintain confidentiality.

Bookcases

CONSIDERATIONS

- Position each bookcase so that it can be accessed easily by those who will be using it, whether it is the teacher, groups of students, or individual students.
- Bookcases and other shelving units can be used for many different purposes in a classroom, including the following:
  - Teacher resource books
  - Classroom library
  - Student books
  - Dictionaries
  - Games

Small Group Instruction Area

It is advantageous to have a designated area, often with a kidney-shaped table, where the teacher, an aide, or a volunteer can work with a small group of students.

CONSIDERATIONS

- Equip the small group instruction area with supplies and materials to facilitate the activities of the groups that work there.
- Position the table and adult's chair where the whole class can be seen and monitored.
- The adult's chair faces the class, and the student chairs face the adult.
- The small group instruction area can be used for many different activities, including the following:
  - Small group discussion
  - Specific skill work
  - Project assistance
  - Writing assistance
  - Writing conferences
  - Portfolio review
  - Assessments
  - Conferences

Learning Centers

Designated areas for students to explore activities across the curriculum—beyond whole class instruction—greatly enrich the learning experience.

CONSIDERATIONS

- Consider how many learning centers you would like to have in your classroom.
- Start with one learning center, and add more as you feel comfortable.
- Position a learning center so that it is easy to monitor.
- Make sure that any computer monitors are clearly visible so that you can monitor student activity.
- Have all necessary supplies and materials easily accessible.
- Learning centers can include, but are not limited to, the following:
  - Writing Center
  - Publishing Center
  - Math Center
  - Science Center
  - Social Studies Center
  - Computer Center
  - Listening Center
  - Art Center
  - Painting Center
  - Clay Table
  - Rug Games and Activities

Storage Space and Supplies

Keep your closets and cabinets well stocked and well organized.

CONSIDERATIONS

- Request supplies for the beginning of the year from the school office.
- Find or purchase supplies elsewhere that are not available through the school office.
- Frequently used supplies should be easily accessible.
- Supplies used only occasionally can be stored out of the way.
- Consider labeling the shelves or drawers where supplies are kept, so that it is easier to put everything in the right place.
- Consider using plastic containers with lids for storage. These are often available at dollar stores or local supermarkets.

Textbooks and
Supplemental Curricular Materials

Textbooks and supplemental instructional kits and supplies for the adopted curriculum must be kept where they are easily available to you, but do not clutter the student space in the classroom.

CONSIDERATIONS

- Inventory all curricular materials.
- Keep all curricular materials readily accessible.
- Consider organizing textbooks and supplemental curricular materials by curricular area.
- Designate a bookcase (or an individual bookshelf or closet shelf) for each curricular area.

Equipment

23
Equipment
Inventory

CONSIDERATIONS

- Inventory all equipment.
- Store equipment in a secure location when it's not in use, such as in designated space in a closet.
- Establish a place for equipment use near power outlets, an Internet connection, Smart Boards, or screens, depending on the specific equipment.

Communication with Parents

Communicating with parents is extremely important. The more you communicate with your students' parents, the more support you are likely to have from them. We discuss a variety of formats for communicating with parents.

CONSIDERATIONS

- Keep parents up-to-date on school and classroom policies.
- Inform parents regularly about what is happening in the classroom.
- Communicate with parents often about their own child.

Welcome Letter

Sending a simple welcome letter home with students on the first day of school gets the school year off to a good start.

CONSIDERATIONS

- Introduce yourself to the parents.
- Outline basic procedures and expectations.
- Ask other teachers who send out a welcome letter to share their ideas with you.
- Obtain office approval for the welcome letter before sending it home.
- Information in a welcome letter could include the following:
  - Information about yourself as the teacher
  - Classroom information, such as schedules and procedures
  - School information, such as policies
  - Reminders for parents, including ways they can assist—both at home and at school

79
Welcome Letter
(sample, blank)

Parent Newsletter

A newsletter keeps parents informed and creates a sense of community.

53
Newsletter
(sample, blank)

CONSIDERATIONS

- Send a newsletter home to parents on the first day of school, or at least within the first week of school.
- Establish a newsletter schedule, such as once a week, and stick to it. A parent newsletter is an excellent way of communicating with parents on a regular basis.
- Use the parent newsletter to demonstrate that your classroom is well organized and is functioning well.
- Get approval from the school office before sending out a newsletter.
- Try a monthly or quarterly newsletter if it is too overwhelming to prepare one more frequently.
- Create a template, and then simply change the content for each newsletter. It's important to make the parent newsletter simple to produce.
- Make the parent newsletter exciting and informative. You want parents to look forward to reading each issue—not disregard it.
- Use the parent newsletter to keep parents informed about your curriculum and your goals for the year.
- Share your focus for the classroom in the parent newsletter, and it will be easier for parents to support you at home.
- Design the parent newsletter with a layout that includes the following elements:
  - Five to eight ideas
  - Two to three columns, or four to six sections
  - School logo
- The content of a parent newsletter could include the following:
  - Teacher contact information
  - Expectations
  - Classroom rules and boundaries; a classroom Bill of Rights
  - Homework protocol
  - Weekly spelling list (10 words for grades K–2, 20 words for grades 3–6)
  - Recommended reading
  - List of books for independent reading
  - Appropriate book report titles
  - List of school-approved recess and lunch snacks
  - Notices for upcoming curriculum nights (such as Literacy Night, Science Night, and Math Night).
  - Upcoming field trips

- Technology websites relevant to current learning
- Current children-friendly movies in theaters or on DVD
- Wish list for materials needed in the classroom

Weekly Homework Sheet and Weekly Lesson Overview

Keep parents informed about their child's weekly academic work with a weekly homework sheet or a weekly lesson overview that shows assigned homework for each day of the week.

CONSIDERATIONS

- Use a template to customize weekly communications with parents.
- Add a motivational quote.
- Include a signature area where a parent signs off when the homework is completed.
- Be flexible. Plans can—and often do—change. Just have students make a note of any changes on their weekly homework sheet.

75, 76
Weekly Lesson
Overviews

73, 74
Weekly
Homework

Weekly Assessment

A weekly assessment that includes the week's spelling test and a report on behavior for the week can be sent home on Fridays for parents to review and sign.

CONSIDERATIONS

- Use a template to customize weekly communications with parents.
- Explain weekly assessment procedures to parents before referring to them in a first parent newsletter or at Back to School Night.
- Be consistent.

71, 72
Weekly
Assessment

A Proactive Approach to Behavior Management

Behavior management in the classroom is key to accomplishing the goals you have for your class. Because handling behavior issues in the classroom potentially takes a lot of classroom time, it is important to be prepared so that any issues that arise can be handled quickly.

CONSIDERATIONS

- Remember that young people are finding their place in the world and, more specifically, in your classroom.
- Realize that students will test where your boundaries lie and what buttons they have to push to get your attention.
- Understand that students need simple and concrete directions that have reasonable and realistic consequences.
- Realize that some of the more typical misbehavior is easy to redirect and manage.
- Be assertive. Your students should know that you are strong and consistent, and that you mean what you say.
- Avoid a nonassertive style of teaching where the children take control.
- Establish standards of behavior that are reasonable, necessary, comprehensible, and consistent with school rules.
- Let your students participate in classroom organization and rule planning so that they are just as invested in it as you are.

Types of Classroom Misbehavior

There are many different types of misbehavior that teachers have to deal with in a typical classroom, including the following:

- Inattention
- Apathy
- Off-task chatter
- Defiance of authority
- Moving around the room without permission
- Disrupting others
- Lying, stealing, or cheating
- Mischief
- Fighting
- Sexual harassment

Working with Students to Avoid Misbehavior

CONSIDERATIONS

- Establish a positive approach for responding to misbehavior. Involve the students whenever possible.
- Make sure that you spend more time teaching than tending to inappropriate behavior.
- Keep students focused on the lesson by making sure that your instruction is both relevant and participatory.
- Understand your students' learning styles, interests, and needs so that you can better reach them by tapping into what they like and how they learn best.
- Treat all students equally. Show fairness by calling on students randomly so that everyone gets a turn.
- Allow those who struggle to have an opportunity to respond to questions that they can answer.
- Find out the causes of inappropriate behaviors.
- Ask experienced teachers how they handle specific behavior situations.
- Involve parents whenever possible. They can be your best resource for strategies that have worked at home, as well as in previous years in the classroom.

21
Conflict
Resolution Slip

Creating a Comfortable Classroom

If you want your students to be open to new information and willing to take academic risks when they come to school each day, you must create an atmosphere where they are comfortable enough to allow this to happen.

CONSIDERATIONS

- Create a safe environment for learning and sharing.
- Explain why you are teaching what you are teaching, and encourage a sense of purpose in the learning experience.
- Try to make your instruction a joyful and satisfying experience for your students.
- Get to know your students both inside and outside the classroom, including the following information about them:
  - Interests
  - Backgrounds
  - Learning styles
  - Fears about learning
- Work to develop personal relationships with your students based on mutual trust.
- Encourage students to exercise self-control and to take responsibility for their actions.
- Reinforce the understanding that there are no excuses for inappropriate behavior.

65
Student Interest
Survey

Behavior Management Ideas

No matter how much you do, there are moments when students test the boundaries. It is important for you to be prepared for those moments—and to act positively.

CONSIDERATIONS

- Involve students in creating classroom rules and consequences.
  - They are more invested in the process and the end results when they have been involved in it from the beginning.
  - It allows you to say, "You *chose* this consequence by breaking this standard of behavior."
- "Catch" students doing the right thing.
  - Call attention to a student who is doing the right thing, especially if that student is one who often tests boundaries.
  - Positive reinforcement encourages students to continue appropriate behavior.

- Be consistent.
  - When a teacher shows that he or she is not always assertive, the students know they can push the boundaries.
  - Classroom rules and consequences must apply to everyone. Students have an acute sense of fairness, and they pick up on inequities very quickly.
- Be flexible.
  - You want to maintain consistency, but it's also important to let students have input, and you need to be willing to bend from time to time.
  - Be sure to let students know that you are making an exception to be flexible in a specific situation, but that they can't assume it's something you'll do all the time.
- Give immediate written and oral feedback.
  - Students want acknowledgment of their work and confirmation that the work they are doing is valid.
  - Walk around the classroom while students are working, and give them immediate oral feedback.
  - When students turn in written work, be sure to give them written feedback that is specific enough that they know you actually read what you assigned.
  - Never assign work that you don't grade or comment on.
- Circulate.
  - You must circulate throughout the room while students are working individually, in pairs, or in small groups in order to know what each of the students is actually doing.
  - If you give students a task, you must move from student to student during the assigned task in order to know who is working on it and who is not.
  - Circulating serves as an opportunity for you to check in with students, ask questions about the task at hand, and encourage them to complete their work.

07
Behavior Log
08
Behavior
Notification

Communicating Effectively

Good communication skills are imperative if you are to deal successfully with the administrators, teachers, and service personnel on your school campus—in both formal meetings and informal interactions.

CONSIDERATIONS

- Assume the best of everyone.
- Operate with the assumption that everyone has the students' best interests in mind.
- Remember that effective communication is the key to having your suggestions and ideas heard and taken seriously.
- Keep a positive attitude.
- Take time to say "hello," and listen to others as much as possible.
- Practice empathy and understanding. Put yourself in the other person's shoes.

Body Language

Body language—a person's stance and presence—speaks volumes, even if not a word is spoken.

CONSIDERATIONS

- Determine whether your body language is in sync with your message.
- Make sure that your nonverbal signals match your words, so that you communicate clearly and are perceived as being approachable.
- Present yourself so that your posture communicates confidence, rather than making you appear unsure of yourself.
- Keep in mind that different people may perceive you differently: Your body language may be perceived differently by men and women, or by different cultural groups.
- Practice eye contact.

- Analyze your physical proximity to the person you are talking with, how your arms are positioned, and the way your facial features convey what you are thinking.
- Try to stay neutral in professional conversations.

Positive Communication

Interactions that are unassuming and clearly understood will be perceived as positive communication.

CONSIDERATIONS

- Assume a neutral frame of reference when you go into a meeting.
- Don't form an opinion or frame a response before you hear from all of the participants in a meeting (potentially every member of the grade-level team, the parents, the administrators, and the support staff).
- Listen carefully. Misunderstandings usually occur when we don't listen.
- Respond with a coherent, quick, informed, and honest reply.
- Avoid speaking in a negative tone of voice.
- Speak so as to have your ideas acknowledged, rather than disregarded because of a negative attitude.
- Be open to learning. No one enjoys a "know-it-all."

Asking Questions

When in doubt, ask!

CONSIDERATIONS

- Ask about something that you don't understand, or at least make a note about it so you can ask later.
- Don't be afraid to ask for explanations, descriptions, and definitions, or about scenarios being discussed.
- If you ask your question politely, no one will take offense. People will appreciate your interest, and your question will remind them to use teacher-friendly language.

Being Prepared

It is good to show consideration for others in a meeting by having everything you need with you and ready to use.

CONSIDERATIONS

- Demonstrate your professionalism by being thoroughly prepared for a meeting.
- Prepare a list of questions or comments you want to address in advance. Include problems that need to be discussed and situations you need to have clarified.
- Come to meetings with all the materials you might need, so that the group can adhere to the agenda.

Being on Time

Being on time for a meeting allows all participants to be productive and efficient.

CONSIDERATIONS

- Be on time for all meetings, even if you have to interrupt what you are doing to get there. (An exception might be if a parent has come to see you.)
- Remember that if you are running late, you should excuse yourself to alert whoever is expecting you that you will not arrive on time.
- Realize that because schools run on tight schedules, starting a meeting just five minutes late can throw it into a tailspin, since people may feel the need to rush through it. This is especially true for before-school meetings.
- Avoid causing hard feelings with other people (for example, administrators or fellow teachers), because your late arrival holds up a decision or causes someone else to run late.

Emergency Contact Information

Accidents are inevitable, so you must be prepared with all emergency contact information.

CONSIDERATIONS

- Check with school and/or district offices for copies of their standard emergency card or a comparable form requesting emergency contact information.
- Send the emergency card home with students during the first week of school.
- Know your students' medical history and how to get in touch with parents or guardians during an emergency. This is critical.
- Make sure that parents provide information about any health concerns or allergies.
- Keep a copy of all relevant phone numbers (or a photocopy of the emergency card) easily accessible.
- Determine if it is advisable to provide your personal phone number to parents. Although this is a personal choice, it is not recommended. It is better to provide the school phone number to parents instead.

15
Class Roster

Recommended Emergency Contact Information

- Phone numbers—work, home, cell phone, and a relative's
- Addresses—home, work, and a relative's
- E-mail addresses—parents, guardians, a relative
- Contact information for a close family friend
- Names of people allowed to pick the student up from school (depending on the student's age)
- Health concerns
- Medical conditions
- Allergies
- Special needs

Emergency Precautions

- Never handle blood without gloves.
- Never attempt to move an injured student. Call for help.
- Never give medication to a student. (Only a nurse or designated office staff is authorized to give out medication.)
- Never diagnose an illness or condition.
- Refer a student to the nurse or the office if in doubt about a situation.

Maintaining Student Records

Documentation of each student's progress, attendance, and test scores for each school year is kept in a cumulative record for that student. This information may be kept electronically or it may be stored in a cumulative folder. These records are permanent.

CONSIDERATIONS

- Be aware that the cumulative record for a student contains information about the academic experiences, challenges, and accomplishments of that particular student.
- Check the cumulative record first if you have questions regarding a student.
- Remember that the kind of information included in the cumulative record will vary somewhat by school district.
- Check with your school on policy and procedures with regard to student records.
- Open cumulative records and update them at the beginning of the year.
- Student records include a lot of information, including the following:
  - Student information
  - Curricular information
  - Yearly standardized test scores
  - Individualized Education Plan (IEP) records
  - English Language Development (ELD) levels
  - Academic background
  - Most recent report cards
  - Conference information
  - Teacher comments
  - Other relevant information

Timetable for Maintenance of Student Records

Beginning of the year—Open the cumulative records to update the information.

Throughout the year—Update the cumulative records with conference information, Individualized Education Plans (IEPs), and English Language Development (ELD) level changes.

End of the year—Close the cumulative records for the year with final report cards, attendance, curriculum studied, and comments.

Cumulative Records

CONSIDERATIONS

- Each student's cumulative record is a legal and confidential student education record.
- By law, cumulative records may be viewed only by school officials for whom the viewing of the record is required to fulfill their professional responsibilities. Parents may request access to their child's record in writing, and students over the age of 18 may request access to their own record in writing.
- Check with your school on policies related to cumulative records.
- Keep all information intact, confidential, and safe.
- Electronic cumulative records must be protected on a secure computer. Always log out when you are finished working with cumulative records so that they are left in a secured state.
- Paper versions of cumulative records should be stored in the school's fireproof cabinet at all times, except when school staff is working directly with one or more of the folders.
- A student's cumulative record that is checked out of the cabinet by a staff member should be replaced each night to avoid the possibility of loss.
- Never take students' cumulative records home or leave them in your classroom.
- Use black ink when entering information for paper versions of cumulative records.
- Keep comments professional and positive. Instead of "Wilson hits other children on the playground," note that "Wilson is experiencing difficulty keeping his hands to himself."

56
Report Card/
Cumulative
Record
Comments

Report Cards

A report card is a current record of a student's scores across the curriculum and the behavior observed for the current period.

CONSIDERATIONS

- Many schools now use a standards-based grading system for report cards.
- The standards-based grading system uses a numerical grading scale (4, 3, 2, 1).
- Standards-based report cards convey information about the students' achievement as follows:
  - 4—Exceeds grade-level standards, advanced understanding
  - 3—Meets grade-level standards, proficient understanding
  - 2—Partially meets grade-level standards, basic understanding
  - 1—Does not meet grade-level standards, little understanding
- Older grading systems use letters (A, B, C, D, F) for report cards.
- Educators who use standards-based grading find that it enables them to assign grades based on clearly defined expectations.
- Some parents and students find it difficult to give up letter grades. This is especially true in the upper grades, when students are preparing to apply to colleges.
- Track students' progress regularly. This allows you to be well prepared when it is time to assign grades, and it provides evidence to support the students' scores.
- Use positive, professional comments. This is standard procedure for legal documentation.

07
Behavior Log

- Positive comments are better received by parents, often serving as an opening for conversation.
- The school or district may provide a list of positively phrased comments for you to use.
- Be as realistic as possible on students' report cards, but take care to phrase comments in an appropriate and professional manner.

56
Report Card/
Cumulative
Record
Comments

- Comment on particular skills or achievements for each student, so that parents have more specific information than "Jefferson is doing well in math."
- Failure notices or not-meeting-standards notices should be sent home a few weeks before the reporting period ends. Check to see what the policy is for your school.
- Check with your office about important dates related to report cards and grading, such as the following:
  - Reporting periods
  - Days in the reporting period
  - Warning notice deadline
  - Submission date
  - Conference dates
  - Conference schedule

Looking Down from Above

Grading Methodologies

Anecdotal Notes

Notes and observations about a student's progress can be kept as anecdotal notes.

CONSIDERATIONS

- Make anecdotal notes each day about several of your students.
- Use Post-it Notes for anecdotal notes, and place these notes in students' individual folders or transfer them to the student log.
- Refer to anecdotal notes when conferencing with parents and/or assigning grades.

Student Portfolios

Collections of a student's best work, chosen by the student, are collected in student portfolios.

CONSIDERATIONS

66
Subject
Portfolio

80
Writing
Portfolio

- Have students select their best work from among their writing, math, science, social studies, and art activities for inclusion in either subject portfolios or a single comprehensive portfolio.
- Share student portfolios at conferences and/or referral meetings.
- Refer to student portfolios when assigning grades, both for the reporting period and for progress reports.

Variety of Assessments

Both formal and informal assessments demonstrate mastery of grade-level standards.

CONSIDERATIONS

- Work with different types of assessments to provide multiple samples of mastery to evaluate. Limiting assessment to just one type isn't fair to the student.
- Remember that most curricular programs have assessments embedded in them as a resource.
- Check with the school office to learn how your district handles periodic assessments.
- Find out how other teachers at your grade level handle assessments.
- Don't overwhelm yourself or your students with too many assessments.
- Plan ahead. Don't try to cram several assessments into the week just before your reporting period ends.

Teacher-Parent-Student Conferences

Regular conferences with the teacher, the parent, and the student are held during the year to discuss each student's progress.

CONSIDERATIONS

- Find out how often your school or district expects you to hold teacher-parent-student conferences. A typical conference schedule will include three teacher-parent-student conferences during the school year: (1) at the beginning of the school year, or the first reporting period, (2) in the middle of the school year, or the second reporting period, and (3) at the end of the school year, or the last reporting period.
- Set up a schedule for your teacher-parent-student conferences. Conferences typically last 15 to 30 minutes.
- Offer parents a selection of time slots. Be flexible, because parents often have to schedule their conference time around work hours, or they may have to leave work to attend.
- Schedule a phone conference if parents cannot attend a conference in person.
- Remember that when you discuss negative behavior or a low score, you need to make sure to find something positive to say as well.
- Allow students to discuss their progress. This holds them accountable.
- Allow students to demonstrate learned skills (such as reading, working math problems, explaining a science experiment) during the conference time.
- Ask students to identify (1) their biggest accomplishment for this reporting period, (2) an area of weakness for this reporting period, and (3) what they'd like to focus on for the next reporting period.
- Analyze the student's effort, interest, and self-reflection in relation to his or her progress.

18
Conference Calendar

19
Conference Reminder

20
Conference Sign-Up Letter

Retention Request

A request for the retention of a student involves a formal documented procedure reviewed by a committee.

CONSIDERATIONS

- Realize that a student who is unable to achieve grade-level expectancy must be given special consideration.
- Remember that a retention request is a last resort.
- Check with the office about the retention policy and procedures of the district.
- Never attempt to diagnose a student; leave that to a professional.
- Keep evidence of student progress (or lack thereof) on an ongoing basis for use during conferences and possible retention discussions.

57
Retention Checklist

Looking Down from Above

- Consider retention for a student in very specific situations, including the following:
  - The student does not meet grade-level standards in three of the major subjects (reading, math, social studies, science).
  - The student consistently has difficulty completing work in class and/or homework, and academic skills do not seem to improve over time.
  - A variety of instructional strategies and differentiation of instruction have already been applied.
  - The student has been referred to the school's Student Study Team.
  - Interventions have been applied.
  - Conferences have been held with the student, parents, and principal.
- You must have a paper trail of interventions, referrals, parent notifications, and conferences in place.
- Communicate with parents on a regular basis so that a discussion about retention does not come as a surprise.
- Assessment of abilities and needs should be made by a team—the assigned teacher, an administrator, additional qualified teachers, and/or a school site representative, nurse, counselor, or school psychologist.
- Proper remediation or developmental work should always be assigned.
- Every effort should be made to help students overcome their difficulties in the areas of concern.
- Consult with the parents and the student (and perhaps the principal) to ensure full understanding and cooperation with regard to the student's placement.
- If retention is approved and a recommendation is made, a follow-up meeting is usually scheduled at which the parent has the ultimate approval authority.

504 Plan

Students with disabilities are eligible for a 504 Plan, which is a planning document based on Section 504 of the Rehabilitation Act of 1973 (with additional protections under the Americans with Disabilities Act of 1990).

CONSIDERATIONS

- "Disability" in a 504 Plan refers to a "physical or mental impairment, which substantially limits one or more major life activities." This may include physical impairments, illnesses, communicable diseases, chronic conditions (such as asthma, allergies, or diabetes), injuries, learning disorders, and communication problems.
- A 504 Plan includes modifications and accommodations for the delivery of instruction to enable students to perform at the same level as their peers—to level the playing field for them.
- The Rehabilitation Act and the Americans with Disabilities Act are civil rights laws.

- Consult with the special education resource teacher or an administrator to review the needs of the 504 Plan students who are assigned to you.
- Know the background and needs of your 504 Plan students.
- Develop appropriate education plans for these students, providing for their needs and accommodations.

IEP (Individualized Education Plan)

Students receiving resource services are eligible for assistance through an IEP, which is a planning document used in combination with the classroom teacher's daily and long-range planning to meet their needs.

CONSIDERATIONS

- Students with an IEP have unique needs and goals that must be acknowledged and planned for.
- The goal of an IEP is to support the student so that he or she will be able to function as effectively as possible in a general education classroom.
- Students with an IEP are most often placed in a general education classroom. Their instruction involves program modifications together with additional support from the special education resource teacher.
- Students with an IEP may leave the classroom at a designated time every day to work with a resource teacher.
- Ask in the school office or check with other teachers to find out how your school district handles IEPs.
- Review IEPs for students who are assigned to you. Resource and special education teachers or your administrator can answer questions you may have about specific goals in the IEP.
- Your planning should reflect accommodations to meet the IEP goals.
- Details of an IEP are typically noted in the teacher's daily and short-range plans.
- IEP goals are reviewed every reporting period, and they are adjusted or modified as needed.
- IEP goals should be shared and discussed at parent conferences along with report cards. Typically a copy of the goals and the student's progress is sent home with each report card.
- IEPs are filed in the student's cumulative record.
- If more educational support is needed, students may be placed in a special education classroom with both direct and indirect support from special education teachers and support staff.

Homework

Homework is a review of the skills and standards that were presented in the instruction during the school day. It is meant to reinforce the learning of the material and to offer additional independent practice.

CONSIDERATIONS

73, 74
Weekly
Homework

- Determine the types of homework assignments to send home with your students based on many factors about this particular group of children, including the following:
  - Grade level
  - Special needs students
  - Advanced learners
  - ELLs (English language learners)
- Realize that students will have just spent six to seven hours with you in the school setting.
- Be cognizant of the level of support that students will have at home for help and encouragement with homework assignments.
- Understand that homework should be a review of what the students learned that day in school.
- Reserve a few assignments for more challenging work or long-term projects, such as book reports, research papers, and science experiments.

Assigning Homework

CONSIDERATIONS

75, 76
Weekly Lesson
Overview

- Operate on the premise that homework is an extension of what students learned in class during the day—not new material.
- Assign homework that is challenging yet attainable—not busy work.
- Include a variety of subject areas without overwhelming the students.
- Assign homework only on Monday through Thursday.

- Consider including the following in your students' nightly assignments:
  - Time to read a book at their instructional level
  - Math review, including a few challenging problems
  - Writing, spelling, and/or grammar exercises
  - Science, health, social studies, art, or technology assignment—but not all of them at once
- Avoid giving homework packets on a Monday that aren't turned in until Friday. This doesn't take into account growth during the week, and it doesn't allow you to differentiate homework based on the students' needs.
- Encourage library visits, Internet exploration or games, long-term research projects, and book reports as weekend activities.
- Never assign homework that you won't actually grade, or for which you won't give your students detailed, immediate feedback. When you don't grade students' work, they are less invested and interested in completing it.
- Develop a homework policy that makes it clear that by not completing homework, students are making the choice to miss a field trip, a special assembly, or a special activity. They will finish their assignments while other students are participating in that activity.
- Include a section in your homework policy that gives students a way to catch up on homework assignments and provides a deadline for completing it (such as by the end of the week or by a specified date).
- Remind students frequently about your homework policy, and offer them opportunities to complete missing assignments.
- Keep parents up-to-date about homework assignments, either by e-mail or by sending a note home. You could also post the homework on your teacher website and list it in a weekly newsletter to the parents.
- Get parents involved early—it avoids controversy later. It's important for parents to know what will be expected so that they can ask questions before the assignments are due.
- Remember that the modern family often keeps a busy, hectic schedule.
- Get parents' input. Find out how much time they are able to devote to helping their child with homework in the evening, and ask what kind of homework they think should be assigned to their children. Use this information as a guide.
- Keep in mind that many students come from households with several children at different grade levels. Consider the real-life circumstances of your students and the feasibility of students being able to complete one to two hours of homework at night.

Homework Chart

33
Homework
Tracker

A homework chart allows you to track completed homework assignments and holds students accountable. It provides many ways to help you and your students be more aware of homework assignments, including the following:

- Tracks assignments that have been turned in on time
- Reminds you and your students which assignments are due and when
- Is a visual alert to missing assignments so that students have time to make them up before the week ends
- Is a good reference for you when completing progress reports at the end of the week

CONSIDERATIONS

- Use a poster-board chart with small boxes where you can note specific assignments and record completed work with a pen or stickers.
- Consider cutting the completed chart into strips and sending each student's strip home at the end of the month. This is especially effective when stickers are used to track homework.

Recommended Minutes of Homework per Day

Kindergarten—15 to 20 minutes
Grade 1—30 to 35 minutes
Grade 2—30 to 35 minutes
Grade 3—35 to 45 minutes
Grade 4—35 to 45 minutes
Grade 5—50 to 60 minutes
Grade 6—15 minutes for each academic class or 30 minutes for each two academic classes
Grades 7 and 8—30 minutes for each academic class or 60 minutes for each two academic classes
Grades 9 through 12—40 minutes for each academic class

Working with Aides and Volunteers

Classroom aides and volunteers can be real assets to the classroom, if you are organized and prepared with a structured routine for them to follow.

CONSIDERATIONS

02
Aide/Volunteer
To-Do List

- Orient aides and volunteers to their space, their role, and the activities they will be helping with.
- Treat your classroom aides and volunteers with respect.
- Teach aides and volunteers the skills they will need for their work in your classroom—skills that they may be unfamiliar with or that they might not have not worked with recently. In order to avoid confusion on the part of your students, you will want the aide or volunteer to teach and/or review material in the same way you would.
- Have needed supplies organized and readily available.
- Never leave students alone with an aide or volunteer (they are not credentialed). *You* are licensed and legally responsible for your students.
- Remember that aides and volunteers have a special role; they should be involved in more than just making copies for your class.
- Follow school and/or district policy on having an aide or volunteer in your classroom.
- Ask other teachers at your grade level how they maximize aide and volunteer time in their classrooms.

Classroom Aide

- Remember that the role of a classroom aide is to help you and to make your job easier.
- Take advantage of aides being able to help students—individually or in small groups—to reinforce taught skills.
- Give aides a focus and provide them with a routine.
- Avoid, as much as possible, having aides simply do paperwork and record keeping.
- Learn from the aides in your classroom. Many classroom aides have been in classrooms longer than you have been, and they are experienced in discipline, grading, working in small groups, and more.
- Maintain professional boundaries, because *you* are still the teacher.

Classroom Volunteer

- Check with the office about the correct protocol and/or procedures for having a volunteer in your classroom.
- Make sure that your volunteers have the required district and/or school clearance, which may include a TB test.
- Have volunteers sign in and sign out at the office; they should wear appropriate identification.
- Start volunteers off slow, because many of them have had little or no experience in a classroom setting before.
- Check in with volunteers frequently, and monitor them. As they feel more comfortable, you can give them more responsibility.
- Be very appreciative of anyone who volunteers time in your classroom.
- Consider the following as potential volunteers:
  - Parents
  - Friends
  - College students
  - Members of the local community
  - Employees of local businesses

Suggested Activities

Activities that an aide or volunteer can do to support you in the classroom include the following:

- Reviewing a lesson
- Reading to students
- Listening to students read aloud
- Reading comprehension (asking students to explain what they've read)
- Building words from letter cards (lower grades)

- Assisting students with the writing process
- Practicing dictation with students (reading words and sentences that students write down)
- Book reports
- Handwriting practice
- Math facts
- Counting and sorting (lower grades)
- Science activity
- Social studies activity
- Art activity supervision
- Helping with online research
- Educational games

Taking Tests:
Preparation and Strategies

Test-taking and assessments are an important part of education. Preparing your students by teaching them specific strategies to use, as well as the material the tests are based on, is essential to their success.

CONSIDERATIONS

- Use assessments and tests to assist you in your evaluation of your students' progress and needs over time.
- Help students use assessments and tests to gauge their level of mastery.
- Help parents monitor their child's progress with assessments and tests.
- Make use of many different forms of tests—from the Friday spelling test and the unit math exam to yearly standardized tests.
- Make sure your students understand that good test-taking is a skill—and that they need to learn it.

Test-Taking Tips for Students

You can help your students tremendously by teaching them how to approach testing in general, as well as how to approach specific types of questions.

- Tell students to relax and do the best they can.
- Remind students to listen carefully to the instructions and to read the directions and each question carefully.
- Suggest that students might want to initially skip over questions they don't know. First, they should answer the questions they know, and then they can tackle the harder ones later. Getting a few questions right early helps build confidence and reduces stress.
- Explain the importance of using time wisely. If students get stuck on a question, encourage them to make the best guess and move on.

- Tell students to attempt to answer all of the questions and not to leave any question blank.
- Help students be aware of key words such as "all," "now," "always," "never," "only," and "exactly" in test questions.
- Tell students to pay attention to what the question is asking for: "least to greatest" or "greatest to least," for example.
- Remind students to look for information in some questions that may be helpful in answering other questions.
- Help students remember to watch for negative words, such as "not," "no," and "never."
- Suggest that for questions based on long reading passages, students might want to preview the questions first and then read the passage with a greater knowledge about what they are looking for.
- Remind students not to skip the longest answer for multiple-choice questions—it should be considered as well.
- If students are taking a Scantron test, remind them to check the number of the question they are answering and make sure that it matches the number on the Scantron.
- Tell students to eliminate ridiculous answers or answers that don't make any sense early, so they can narrow the field of possible answers.
- Remind students that if they are fatigued during the test, they should stop, take a breath, count to ten, and then continue.
- Encourage students not to change an answer unless there is a good reason to do so. (The first choice is usually correct.)
- Encourage students to stay focused on the test, even if other students finish early.

Preparation Tips for Teachers

- Have extra pencils or pens, scratch paper, rulers, a door sign that announces "We are testing," and any other needed materials available on the day of the test.
- If your class is disappointed after taking a test, reassure them that there will be plenty of opportunities to improve.

Preparation Tips for Parents

Parents can help their children be better prepared to take tests if they are aware of some of the ways they can support their children. Share the following tips with the parents of your students:

- Make sure your child gets a good night's sleep before a test.
- Make sure your child eats properly the day of a test.
- Maintain a calm home environment, and avoid unnecessary conflicts—especially on the morning of a test.
- Make sure that your child is present and on time for testing.

- Remind your child that a test is important.
- Wish your child good luck on the test.
- Tell your child that you believe in his or her abilities.
- Encourage your child to do his or her best.
- If the test is on a subject that you can review with your child, you may certainly help your child review at home.
- If your child is too ill to attend on a testing day, please call or e-mail the teacher and, if possible, schedule a make-up test before school during the next couple of days.

Strategies for Yearly Standardized Tests

Tests are an important way to review the skills learned. The following are strategies that can help your students during test-taking year-round, and especially during the yearly standardized tests:

- Have your students practice using scratch paper during test-taking. Fold a sheet of plain newsprint in half three times, creating eight boxes. Have students practice learning to copy and solve problems on scratch paper in an organized manner. Make sure they do this throughout the year so that they are comfortable with it when it's time for the yearly standardized tests.
- For tests involving long reading passages, have your students practice previewing questions, underlining key information, reading the passage, and underlining the answers in the passage.
- For math review (upper grades), write a standard and a definition on the front of an index card, and give an example on the back. Have students review and study these standards.
- Have your students practice reading comprehension and math word problems throughout the year.
- Have your students practice word attack skills.
  - Lower grades—decoding, blending
  - Upper grades—looking for prefixes, suffixes, and other hints that may help a student derive meaning; looking at the use of a word in context
- Practice grammar throughout the year with your students and review it using index cards (upper grades). Write the skill on the front of the card and an example on the back. Have students review and study them.
- Make use of the many test preparation materials that can be found on-line, at teacher supply stores, and at your school site. Practice with these materials throughout the year so that students are familiar and comfortable with them.

Organizing Students in Line

Your line-up, while it may sound insignificant, sets the tone for classroom conduct. An orderly line reflects well on you and your class.

CONSIDERATIONS

- Teach students to get organized and lined up quickly.
- Make students aware that this can be a safety issue if they are exiting the building quickly during a fire drill or an emergency.
- Practice lining up.
- Emphasize that students should be able to hear the teacher's voice at all times.

Methods
ABC Order

Students line up in alphabetical order by last name. Used at the beginning of the school year, this method is a great way for students to get to know one another's names.

- Gather students in front of you.
- Ask the students to line up alphabetically by first or last name.
- Practice this for the first couple of weeks of school.

SUGGESTION

- Assign each of the students a number, so that they can line up in numerical order.

Academic Line-Up

Students state a fact they have learned as they line up.

- Draw names randomly (from your deck of cards or popsicle sticks) when it's time to excuse students to line up.
- Ask them to tell you one thing they learned from the lesson that day.
- As they share out, the students can line up.

SUGGESTION

- Have students tell you facts from other areas of learning, such as the name of the capital for a given state, the name of a president, or a math fact.

Birthdays

Children line up as their birthday month is called.

Colors

Students line up according to what color they are wearing.

- Ask for the students who are wearing something red to line up, then call for those students wearing blue, then green, and so on.

SUGGESTION

- Use different categories, such as articles of clothing (pants, skirts), physical characteristics (short hair, long hair), and so on.

I Spy

The teacher spies something and students line up as they guess the object.

- Give the students a clue about the object, for example, "I spy something with a right angle."
- The students respond, and as students are called on and give their response, they line up.
- Do this in pairs or by table groups to save time.

Individual, Pair, or Table Behavior

Students line up based on behavior.

- Excuse students to line up based on their having materials put away or demonstrating specified appropriate behavior. For example, you might say, "I will excuse a table when everyone at the table is prepared to line up."

Rules and Consequences

Students line up by reviewing classroom rules and consequences.

- Ask students to give one classroom rule, or one consequence that results from abiding by a rule or breaking it.
- Students line up when they give a correct answer.

SUGGESTIONS

- Present a scenario, and have students tell which rule was broken and how they can avoid breaking it in the future. As these are responded to, students can line up.
- Do this in pairs or by table groups to save time.

Stretching Line-Up

After the students have lined up quietly, have them spread out a bit so they can do some calming stretches before heading out to recess or lunch, or at the end of the day.

Looking Down from Above

Rubrics

A rubric measures your students' success based on a four-point scale. Rubrics provide a great way to assess your students, while setting out clear expectations for them and for you.

CONSIDERATIONS

- Select three to five specific goals or target skills that you want an assignment to demonstrate.
- Students are scored on a scale of 1 to 4 (with 4 being the highest), based on their level of achievement for each skill.
- Establish clear expectations so that students understand exactly what they need to achieve to earn a specific score.
- Show your students how the rubric helps explain *why* they received a specific score.

Rubric Scale

4—All ultimate goals achieved (terms to use: *all, complete,* etc.)

3—Most goals achieved, excellent attempt with a few minor corrections (terms to use: *most, no more than two mistakes,* etc.)

2—Some goals achieved, attempt recognized, but needs support (terms to use: *some, part, partial, a few, three or four errors,* etc.)

1—Minimal goals achieved, needs a great deal of support (terms to use: *little or no evidence, minimal, none, more than four errors,* etc.)

- Limit goals per assignment to no more than three to five (for lower grades, you might have even fewer).
- Write goals so that they are explicit and specific (especially for grades 2 and above; for lower grades, they might be more general).
- Communicate the goals to your students verbally, and explain them to your students.
- Use graphics like smiley faces for students in the lower grades. Use more elaborate graphics for students in the upper grades.

58, 59, 60, 61
Rubrics

EXAMPLE 1

Goal—Students use correct ending punctuation.

Rubric

4—*All* sentences have the correct ending punctuation.

3—*Most* of the sentences have the correct ending punctuation. (no more than two errors)

2—*Some* of the sentences have correct ending punctuation. (no more than three or four errors)

1—There is *little or no evidence* of ending punctuation. (more than four errors)

EXAMPLE 2

Goal—Students complete a coloring sheet.

General rubric (lower grades)

4—Perfect score, can't ask for more. Look at me, I am a four.

3—Almost perfect, look at me. Doing great, I am a three.

2—Still much to do, makes me a two. But I can do it, I'll show you.

1—I have just begun. With hard work, I'll get it done, but for now I'm just a one.

Website Resources

The Internet is an excellent resource for practically everything you do in your classroom. When you need ideas for planning and delivering instruction or how to play certain games, look online—it's probably there!

CONSIDERATIONS

- Consider posting or bookmarking student-approved websites in your computer center.
- Send a list of approved websites home for parents to use when their child finishes homework early or on weekends.
- Preview sites before using them in your classroom or recommending them to parents. Try them out, and make sure that they work for you and further your educational goals.
- Expand the list of approved websites with the help of your students. They enjoy finding new sites and are probably aware of sites that you don't yet know about. (At school, a firewall should protect your students from inappropriate websites.)
- Ask other teachers for websites that they find helpful and/or useful.

Helpful Teacher Websites

atozteacherstuff.com

FOCUS   Online teacher resources

RESOURCES Lesson plans, thematic units, teacher tips, discussion forums for teachers, downloadable teaching materials, eBooks, printable worksheets, emergent reader books, themes

FEE   Free

edhelper.com

FOCUS   Useful educational resources

RESOURCES Lesson plans and worksheets across the curriculum

FEE $19.00 per year for a basic subscription, $39.98 per year for an "everything" subscription

teachertube.com

FOCUS   Online community for sharing instructional videos

RESOURCES Professional development with teachers teaching teachers, videos designed for students to learn a concept or skill

FEE   Free

enchantedlearning.com

FOCUS   Teacher resources across the curriculum

RESOURCES Downloadable resources for a variety of lessons

FEE $20.00 per year

teacherweb.com

FOCUS   Website templates for teachers and administrators

RESOURCES Completely customizable and easy-to-use website templates that can be created and updated to suit your personal need for a classroom webpage

FEE $39.00 per year

starfall.com

FOCUS   Reading activities for lower grades

RESOURCES Excellent interactive read-alongs

FEE   Free

abcteach.com

FOCUS   Printable worksheets of all kinds for students in grades Pre-K through 8

RESOURCES Activity pages, PowerPoint presentations, unit ideas, portfolio concepts

FEE $35.00 per year

henryanker.com

FOCUS   Grade K–6 standards-based electronic tests

RESOURCES Standards-based electronic assessment practice for Grades K–6 and excellent links to additional websites

FEE   Free

Favorite Student Websites

tumblebooks.com

FOCUS   Enrichment for independent readers

RESOURCES High-interest material, support for skill-building with a variety of exercises that can be matched with other areas of the curriculum

FEE   Monthly fee if you want it for yourself or the school site, but many public libraries offer it for free

childrenslibrary.org

FOCUS   Children's literature from the world community

RESOURCES   Outstanding books from throughout the world, both historical and contemporary

FEE   Free

bbc.co.uk/schools/typing

FOCUS   Introduction to touch-typing for children aged 7 to 11 years

RESOURCES   Leveled typing challenges (4 levels, each of which is divided into 3 stages)

FEE   Free

mathisfun.com

FOCUS   Resources for math

RESOURCES   Definitions of math terms, math applications, interactive math practice

FEE   Free

meetmeatthecorner.org

FOCUS   Virtual field trips to meet fascinating people from all over the world

RESOURCES   Kid-friendly episodes uploaded every two weeks, links to fun websites, a learning corner with follow-up questions

FEE   Free

coolmath4kids.com

FOCUS   Math games

RESOURCES   Fun, interactive games that reinforce many different math skills

FEE   Free

Templates

The key on pages 194–199 lists the templates available as PDFs on the accompanying CD. The key includes the number of each template, as well as information and instructions for its use. The symbol 💻 next to a template number in the key indicates that the template is also available as a PDF electronic form, which can be filled in on a computer and printed. Adobe Reader is required to open PDFs.

Thumbnails of all templates are reproduced on pages 200–224. The symbol 💻 after a template number on the thumbnail pages has the same meaning as in the key below.

Be sure to set Adobe Reader to highlight the form fields as follows:

Preferences >
Forms >
Highlight Color: ☑ Show border hover color for fields

Note that your filled-in forms cannot be saved on the computer.

A gray arrow at the side edge of a template (for example, ➡) indicates that the template is included with an adjoining template in a multipage PDF.

01 Acronyms and Terms
This basic list of acronyms and terms may be added to as needed.

02 Aide/Volunteer To-Do List
Use this template to plan a session when an aide or volunteer will be assisting students in your classroom.

03 Back to School Night Checklist
Use this checklist to help you prepare for Back to School Night.

04 Back to School Night Invitation
Send this invitation home as a reminder to parents.

05 Back to School Night Sign-In Sheet
Use this sign-in sheet at Back to School Night as a record of parent attendance.

06 Behavior Contract
Complete this form with the student's name and three behavior goals. Circle the faces that correspond to the student's progress.

07 Behavior Log
Use this log to track a student's behavior. Save the log for referral procedures and parent/guardian conferences.

08 Behavior Notification
Fill out this form and send it home as needed.

09 Behavior Tracker
Complete this form with the student's name and the behavior goal of the week. Initial, check, or add a smiley face in the appropriate box as the goal is achieved. Send the form home daily or at the end of the week.

10 Bingo 1
For lower grades. Each student fills in a card with numbers or words from the unit. As the teacher calls out a question, the student covers the answer if it appears on his or her card. The first student to cover three answers in a row (across, down, or diagonally) wins. Ideas for fill-ins are math facts, sight words, synonyms, antonyms, definitions, numbers, and fractions.

11 Bingo 2
For upper grades. Each student fills in a card with numbers or words from the unit. As the teacher calls out a question, the student covers the answer if it appears on his or her card. The first student to cover five answers in a row (across, down, or diagonally) wins. Ideas for fill-ins are math facts, sight words, synonyms, antonyms, definitions, numbers, and fractions.

12 Book Report 1
For lower grades

13 Book Report 2
For upper grades

14 Classroom Door Sign
Cut out this sign and the location cards. Color and laminate the sign and cards. Post the appropriate card on the sign when you are out of the classroom.

🖳 **15 Class Roster**
Use this class roster as a current record of the students in your class. Medical information includes information about allergies, asthma, medications, eyeglasses, and special needs.

🖳 **16 Computer Sign-In Sheet**
Use this sign-in sheet as a means for the students to use the computer in an orderly fashion.

🖳 **17 Computer User Name and Password Log**
Use this log to record students' user names and passwords. For a password, consider using the student's initials plus two-digit birth month and date (for example, smd1230).

🖳 **18 Conference Calendar**
Based on the responses from parents/guardians to the Conference Sign-Up Letter (template #20), assign conference appointments.

19 Conference Reminder
Once conference appointments have been assigned, send one of these reminders home with each student the day before the scheduled conference.

🖳 **20 Conference Sign-Up Letter**
Check with the office for off-limit days and times. Fill in potential dates and times in the first column of this form. Fill in the remainder of the form, sign the letter, and send it home with each student.

21 Conflict Resolution Slip
Students work together to discuss and resolve their conflicts, filling in the slip as they proceed. They then submit the Conflict Resolution Slip to the teacher and share their resolution.

🖳 **22 Daily Schedule Organizer**
List each instructional activity, including the number of minutes mandated for daily instruction in the activity.

🖳 **23 Equipment Inventory**
Include computers, projectors, document readers, and Smart Boards. Save this sheet for the annual school inventory.

🖳 **24 Field Trip Checklist**
Use this checklist to help you prepare for and organize field trip days.

🖳 **25 Field Trip Roster**
Assign student partners, then assign one adult to each group of 10 students. Identify students with medical alerts. Distribute this form to all adults on the trip.

26 First Day Classroom Checklist
Use this checklist to help you prepare your classroom for the first day of school.

27 First Day Student Checklist
Use this checklist to help you prepare materials for your students for the first day of school.

28 First Day Teacher Checklist
Use this checklist to help you prepare your own teacher resources and supplies for the first day of school.

Templates

🖥 **79** Welcome Letter

   A sample Welcome Letter is provided, as well as a blank template.

🖥 **80** Writing Portfolio

   This portfolio cover is updated as written pieces are evaluated.

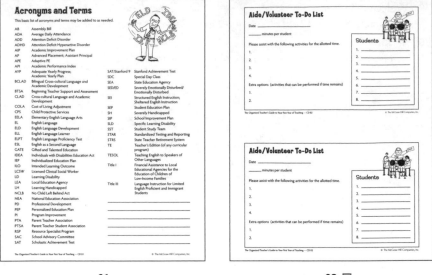

01

Acronyms and Terms

02 🖥

Aide/Volunteer To-Do List

03

Back to School Night Checklist

04 🖥

Back to School Night Invitation

Templates

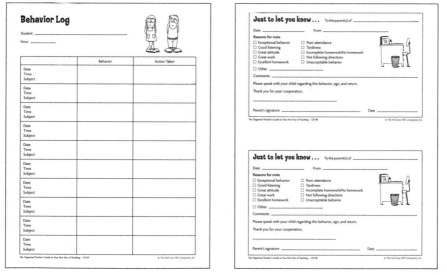

05 🖳
Back to School Night Sign-In Sheet

06 🖳
Behavior Contract

07 🖳
Behavior Log

08
Behavior Notification

Templates

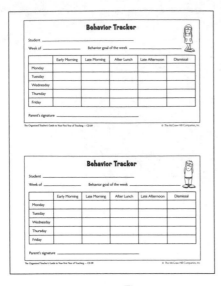

09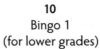
Behavior Tracker

10
Bingo 1
(for lower grades)

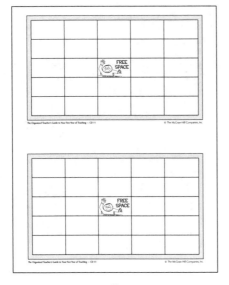

11
Bingo 2
(for upper grades)

12
Book Report 1
(for lower grades)

13
Book Report 2
(for upper grades)

14 🖥️
Classroom Door Sign

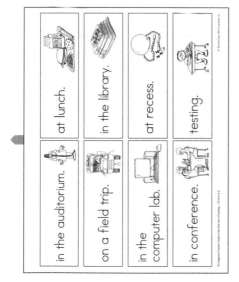

14
Classroom Door Sign

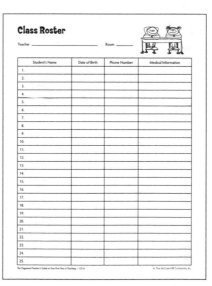

15 🖥️
Class Roster

Templates

Computer Sign-In Sheet

Students sign in and out for a designated period of _____ minutes.

Student's Name	Sign-In Time	Sign-Out Time

The Organized Teacher's Guide to Your First Year of Teaching — CD 16 · © The McGraw-Hill Companies, Inc.

16 🖳
Computer Sign-In Sheet

Computer User Name and Password Log

Teacher _____ Room _____

Student's Name	User Name	Password

The Organized Teacher's Guide to Your First Year of Teaching — CD 17 · © The McGraw-Hill Companies, Inc.

17 🖳
Computer User Name
and Password Log

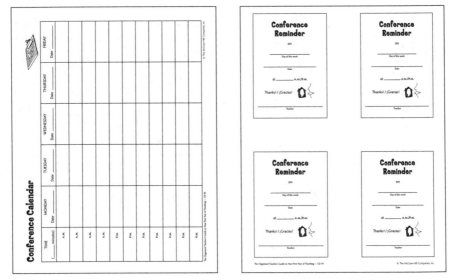

18 🖳
Conference Calendar

19
Conference Reminder

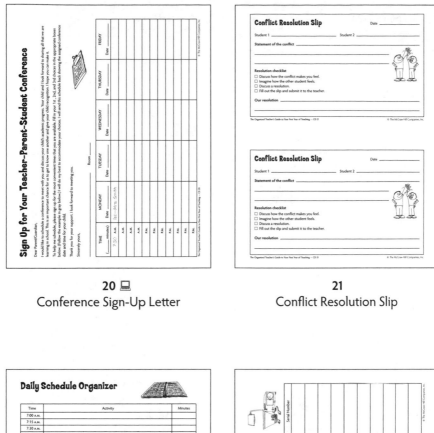

20 🖥
Conference Sign-Up Letter

21
Conflict Resolution Slip

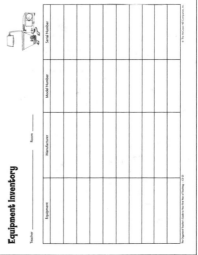

22 🖥
Daily Schedule Organizer

23 🖥
Equipment Inventory

Templates

Field Trip Checklist

24 🖥
Field Trip Checklist

25 🖥
Field Trip Roster

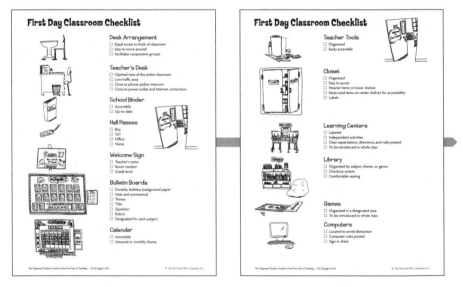

26
First Day Classroom Checklist

26
First Day Classroom Checklist

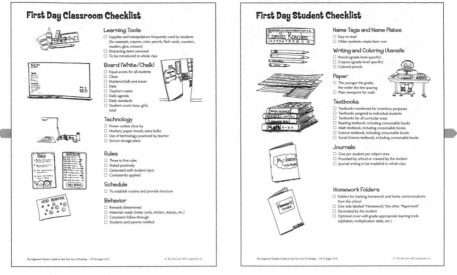

26
First Day Classroom Checklist

27
First Day Student Checklist

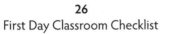

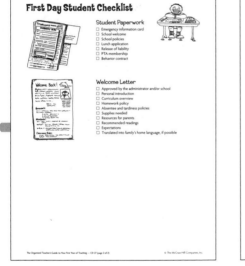

27
First Day Student Checklist

28
First Day Teacher Checklist

Templates

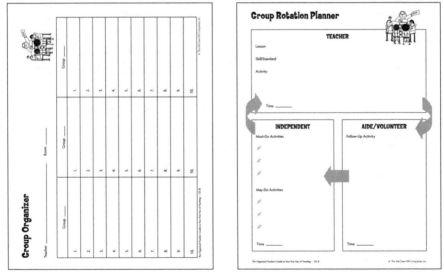

28
First Day Teacher Checklist

29
Formal Evaluation Checklist

30 🖥
Group Organizer

31 🖥
Group Rotation Planner

Templates

32 🖥
Hall Passes

32 🖥
Hall Passes

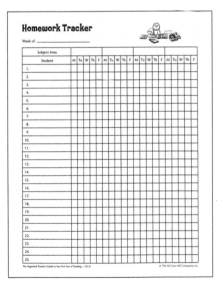

33 🖥
Homework Tracker

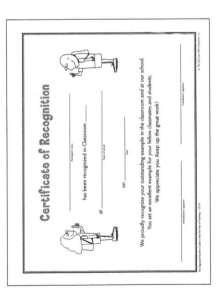

34 🖥
Incentive Certificate 1
(Certificate of Recognition)

Templates

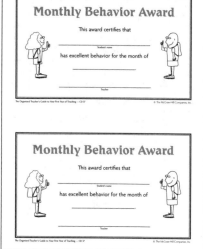

35 💻
Incentive Certificate 2
(Monthly Attendance Award)

36 💻
Incentive Certificate 3
(Weekly Attendance Award)

37 💻
Incentive Certificate 4
(Monthly Behavior Award)

38 💻
Incentive Certificate 5
(Weekly Behavior Award)

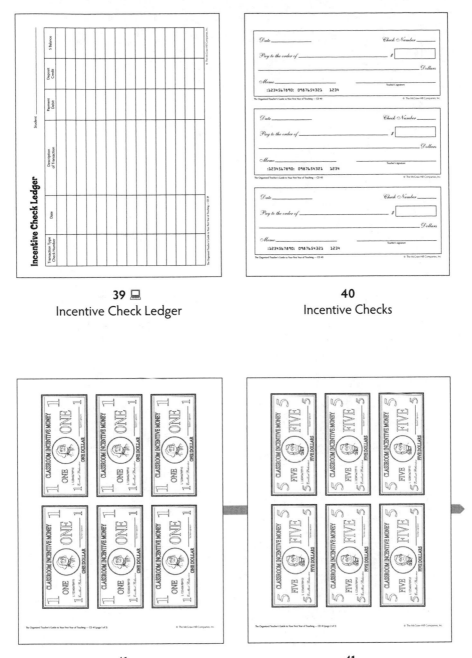

39 🖳
Incentive Check Ledger

40
Incentive Checks

41
Incentive Money

41
Incentive Money

Templates

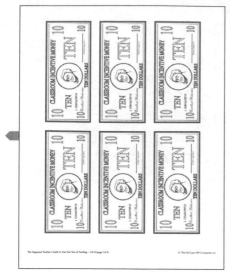

41
Incentive Money

42 💻
Incentive Tickets 1
(Admit One fill-in)

43
Incentive Tickets 2
(Admit One to Ice Cream Party)

44
Incentive Tickets 3
(Admit One to Movie)

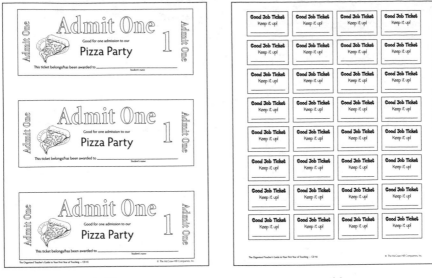

45
Incentive Tickets 4
(Admit One to Pizza Party)

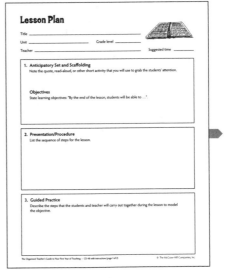

46
Incentive Tickets 5
(Good Job Tickets)

47
Incentive Behavior Log

48
Lesson Plan 1
(with instructions)

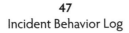

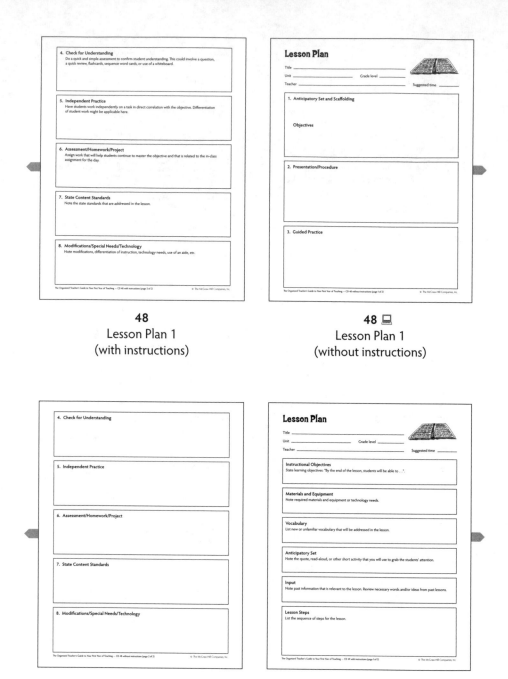

48
Lesson Plan 1
(with instructions)

48
Lesson Plan 1
(without instructions)

48
Lesson Plan 1
(without instructions)

49
Lesson Plan 2
(with instructions)

Templates

Template 1 (top left): Lesson Plan 2 (with instructions)

Guided Practice
Describe the steps that the students and teacher will carry out together during the lesson to model the objective.

Check for Understanding
Do a quick and simple assessment to confirm student understanding. This could involve a question, a quick review, flashcards, sequence word cards, or use of a whiteboard.

Independent Practice
Have students work independently on a task in direct correlation with the objective. Differentiation of student work might be applicable here.

Closure
Review what was learned during the lesson through a series of related questions, discussion about new vocabulary and/or ideas, and a prediction, if applicable.

Modifications/Special Needs/Technology
Note modifications, differentiation of instruction, technology needs, use of an aide, etc.

Assessment/Homework/Project
Assign work that will help students continue to master the objective and that is related to the in-class assignment for the day.

The Organized Teacher's Guide to Your First Year of Teaching — CD 49 with instructions (page 2 of 2)   © The McGraw-Hill Companies, Inc.

49
Lesson Plan 2
(with instructions)

Template 2 (top right): Lesson Plan (without instructions)

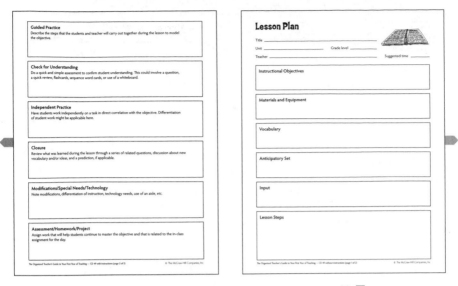

Lesson Plan

Title _____

Unit _____ Grade level _____

Teacher _____ Suggested time _____

Instructional Objectives

Materials and Equipment

Vocabulary

Anticipatory Set

Input

Lesson Steps

The Organized Teacher's Guide to Your First Year of Teaching — CD 49 without instructions (page 1 of 2)   © The McGraw-Hill Companies, Inc.

49 🖥
Lesson Plan 2
(without instructions)

Template 3 (bottom left): Lesson Plan 2 (without instructions)

Guided Practice

Check for Understanding

Independent Practice

Closure

Modifications/Special Needs/Technology

Assessment/Homework/Project

The Organized Teacher's Guide to Your First Year of Teaching — CD 49 without instructions (page 2 of 2)   © The McGraw-Hill Companies, Inc.

49 🖥
Lesson Plan 2
(without instructions)

Template 4 (bottom right): Into-Through-and-Beyond (with instructions)

Into-Through-and-Beyond

Think
What is the "big idea" you want students to be thinking about? What are the essential questions? You may want to post the questions on the board for students to contemplate.

Objectives
What will students learn from this lesson? "By the end of the lesson, students will be able to . . .".

INTO
Provide initial activities that introduce your students to, or prepare them for, the concepts and skills to be covered in the lesson. Connect the "big idea" of the lesson to students' experiences. Have students respond in writing to a prompt or a think-pair-share, or engage in a whole-class discussion. Use predicting strategies, brainstorming, pictures, primary documents, videos, hands-on experiences, question generation, and/or text preview to present content and new vocabulary.

THROUGH
What will you model for your students? To provide the context and content for learning, consider using graphic organizers, analysis and/or summary of text, new vocabulary, double-entry journals or diaries, strategic Post-it Notes, mini whiteboards, small group work, experiments, use of manipulatives, and illustration.

The Organized Teacher's Guide to Your First Year of Teaching — CD 50 with instructions (page 1 of 3)   © The McGraw-Hill Companies, Inc.

50
Into-Through-and-Beyond
(with instructions)

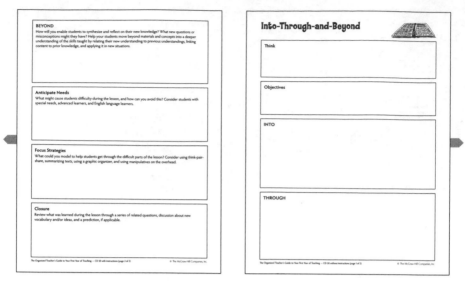

BEYOND
How will you enable students to synthesize and reflect on their new knowledge? What new questions or misconceptions might they have? Help your students move beyond materials and concepts into a deeper understanding of the skills taught by relating their new understanding to previous understandings, linking content to prior knowledge, and applying it in new situations.

Anticipate Needs
What might cause students difficulty during the lesson, and how can you avoid this? Consider students with special needs, advanced learners, and English language learners.

Focus Strategies
What could you model to help students get through the difficult parts of the lesson? Consider using think-pair-share, summarizing texts, using a graphic organizer, and using manipulatives on the overhead.

Closure
Review what was learned during the lesson through a series of related questions, discussion about new vocabulary and/or ideas, and a prediction, if applicable.

Into-Through-and-Beyond

Think

Objectives

INTO

THROUGH

50
Into-Through-and-Beyond
(with instructions)

50 🖥
Into-Through-and-Beyond
(without instructions)

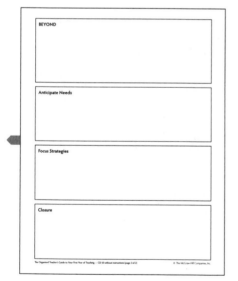

BEYOND

Anticipate Needs

Focus Strategies

Closure

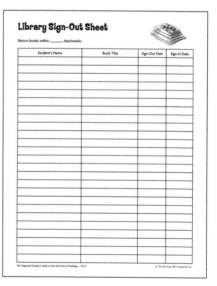

Library Sign-Out Sheet

Return books within _____ days/weeks.

Student's Name	Book Title	Sign-Out Date	Sign-In Date

50 🖥
Into-Through-and-Beyond
(without instructions)

51 🖥
Library Sign-Out Sheet

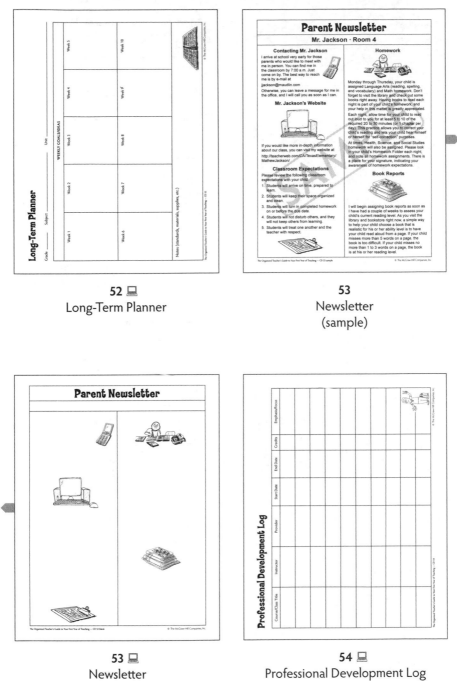

52 💻
Long-Term Planner

53
Newsletter
(sample)

53 💻
Newsletter
(blank)

54 💻
Professional Development Log

Templates

Reading Log

Name _____ to _____ Month _____

Read for _____ to _____ minutes each night, then have an adult sign and date below,
noting the number of minutes of reading time.

Book Title	Parent's Signature	Date	Time

The Organized Teacher's Guide to Your First Year of Teaching – CD 55   © The McGraw-Hill Companies, Inc.

55 🖥️
Reading Log

Report Card / Cumulative Record Comments

Positive Descriptors

Instead of saying …	Say …
Has a bad attitude	Is working to become a more positive learner
Is a bully	Can be assertive with other students
Gets into fights	Has difficulty with self-control
Talks back	Shows little or no respect for authority
Has no friends	Is learning to work cooperatively
Won't talk	Is very shy OR Is developing social skills
Refuses to participate	Has difficulty being an active participant
Talks too much	Is highly sociable
Plays too much	Is easily distracted
Runs around the classroom	Has difficulty staying in his or her seat
Misses school too often	Needs to improve attendance OR Has inconsistent attendance
Is often late	Needs to improve punctuality OR Is working toward improved punctuality
Is messy	Needs to improve neatness OR Is developing neatness
Doesn't complete assignments	Has difficulty staying on task or completing class work
Won't work	Demonstrates low motivation
Can't write a sentence/paragraph	Struggles with sentence/paragraph construction
Can't read	Needs support with reading OR Is having difficulty with word attack skills
Uses poor English	Needs to improve English language acquisition OR Is working toward English language acquisition
Doesn't know math facts	Has not met grade-level standards for math facts ($+ - \times \div$)
Is failing	Is not working at grade-level standards OR Is working below grade-level standards

Positive Key Words

Respectful
Cooperative
Enthusiastic
Highly motivated
Outstanding
Excellent
Demonstrates understanding of …
Is improving
Is doing well
Is working toward mastery of …
Has mastered …
Shows strength in …

The Organized Teacher's Guide to Your First Year of Teaching – CD 56   © The McGraw-Hill Companies, Inc.

56
**Report Card/Cumulative Record
Comments**

Retention Checklist

General Information

☐ Student's name
☐ Grade
☐ Parent's/Guardian's name
☐ Address
☐ Phone
☐ Date of birth
☐ Age (years and months)
☐ Primary language; ELD level, if applicable
☐ Attendance during last three years
☐ Health records (height and weight, medical history)
☐ Vision problem
☐ Speech or language problem
☐ Diagnosed learning disability
☐ Referral services – received
☐ Outside agency support
☐ Teacher evaluation of present social and emotional development
☐ Reason for retention
☐ Evaluation committee – review and recommendations

Evaluation of Present Academic Achievement

☐ Reading level
☐ Math level
☐ Language level
☐ Written work

Previous Attempts to Assist Student

☐ Student's past history in school
☐ Consultation with previous teacher – interventions, observations, academic performance
☐ Frequency
☐ Special education
☐ Speech therapy
☐ Tutoring
☐ Other

Parent Participation

☐ Response from parents
☐ Documentation of communication with parent(s), including dates and times, as noted on report cards,
school retentions, failure notices
☐ Documentation of communication with parent(s) in conferences
☐ Documentation of parent's or guardian's request for retention, including dates and times – written and oral

The Organized Teacher's Guide to Your First Year of Teaching – CD 57   © The McGraw-Hill Companies, Inc.

57
Retention Checklist

Rubric

Name _____

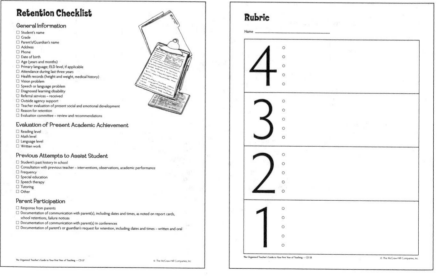

58 🖥️
**Rubric 1
(vertical)**

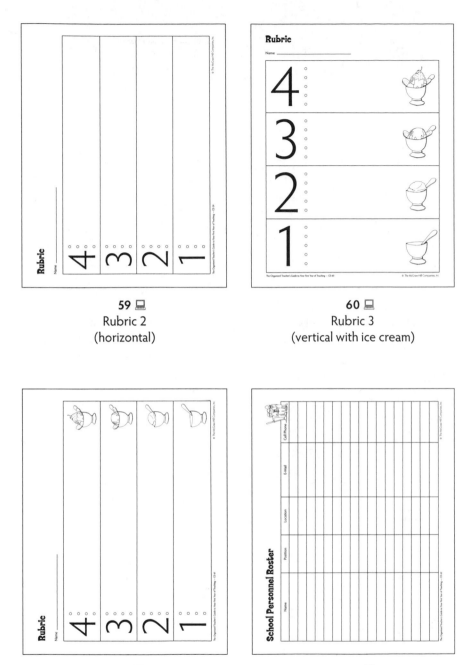

59 🖥
Rubric 2
(horizontal)

60 🖥
Rubric 3
(vertical with ice cream)

61 🖥
Rubric 4
(horizontal with ice cream)

62 🖥
School Personnel Roster

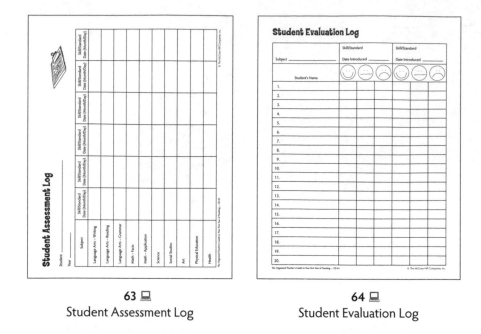

63 🖥
Student Assessment Log

64 🖥
Student Evaluation Log

65
Student Interest Survey

66 🖥
Subject Portfolio

Substitute Teacher Checklist

Teacher
- ☐ Notify the office.
- ☐ Use the district's substitute finder (by telephone or online).
- ☐ Inform another teacher at your grade level.
- ☐ Complete the Substitute Teacher Information sheet (CD 69).
- ☐ Discuss your absence with your students.

Classroom
- ☐ Classroom – clean, orderly, and ready
- ☐ Seating chart, including a map of the desks
- ☐ Student name plates on desks
- ☐ Duty and class schedules
- ☐ List of special schedules or activities for the day
- ☐ Lesson plans – detailed and organized
- ☐ Teacher's editions and other resource books
- ☐ Copies of activity sheets
- ☐ Rules and consequences
- ☐ Referral forms and hall passes
- ☐ Materials – books, rulers, scissors, etc.
- ☐ Supplies – paper, pencils, glue sticks, etc.
- ☐ Emergency exit procedure
- ☐ Emergency backpack or kit
- ☐ List of classroom helpers
- ☐ Classroom policies

Substitute Teacher To-Do List
1. _____
2. _____
3. _____
4. _____
5. _____
6. _____
7. _____
8. _____
9. _____
10. _____

The Organized Teacher's Guide to Your First Year of Teaching — CD 67   © The McGraw-Hill Companies, Inc.

67
Substitute Teacher Checklist

Substitute Teacher Feedback

Name _____ Date _____

Employee number _____ Phone number _____

The Day
Things we accomplished

Things we didn't get to

The Class
Helpful hands

Anecdotal
Concerns and issues

Student's Name	Concern/Behavior	Action Taken

Thanks for your help!

The Organized Teacher's Guide to Your First Year of Teaching — CD 68   © The McGraw-Hill Companies, Inc.

68
Substitute Teacher Feedback

Substitute Teacher Information
Welcome!

Quick Check
- ☐ Lesson plans
- ☐ Clean, orderly classroom
- ☐ Copies of activity sheets

Teacher's name _____ Phone number _____

School overview

School name _____

Address _____ Phone number _____

Principal _____ Vice-Principal _____

Office Manager _____ Ext. _____

Nurse _____ Ext. _____ Room _____

Custodian _____

Teacher's Lounge   Room _____

School starts _____ A.M.   Meet students _____ A.M.

Recess _____ to _____   Students _____

Lunch _____ to _____   Students _____

School ends _____ P.M.   Dismiss students _____ P.M.

Special activities

Date _____ from _____ to _____ Location _____

Date _____ from _____ to _____ Location _____

Responsible student helpers _____

Teacher contacts

Name _____ Grade level _____ Room _____ Ext. _____

Name _____ Grade level _____ Room _____ Ext. _____

Aide _____ Hours _____

Students receiving special services/medical care

Reminders

The Organized Teacher's Guide to Your First Year of Teaching — CD 69   © The McGraw-Hill Companies, Inc.

69 🖥
Substitute Teacher Information

Textbook Inventory

Subject _____

Student's Name	Book Number	Sign-Out Date	Sign-In Date
1.			
2.			
3.			
4.			
5.			
6.			
7.			
8.			
9.			
10.			
11.			
12.			
13.			
14.			
15.			
16.			
17.			
18.			
19.			
20.			
21.			
22.			
23.			
24.			
25.			

The Organized Teacher's Guide to Your First Year of Teaching — CD 70   © The McGraw-Hill Companies, Inc.

70 🖥
Textbook Inventory

Weekly Assessment

Name _____
Date _____

Weekly Spelling List	Behavior
1. _____	
2. _____	Attendance
3. _____	Asistencia □ □
4. _____	Classroom behavior
5. _____	Comportamiento en la clase □ □
6. _____	Playground behavior
7. _____	Comportamiento en la yarda □ □
8. _____	Homework
9. _____	Tarea □ □
10. _____	Work quality
Bonus _____	Cualidad de trabajo □ □
	Spelling _____%
	Deletreo □ □
	Math _____%
	Matemática □ □
	Comments Comentario
	_____
	Parent's signature Firma del padre

Sentence _____
_____
_____

The Organized Teacher's Guide to Your First Year of Teaching — CD 71   © The McGraw-Hill Companies, Inc.

71
Weekly Assessment 1
(for lower grades)

Weekly Assessment

Name _____   Date _____

Weekly Spelling List	Behavior
1. _____	
2. _____	Attendance
3. _____	Asistencia □ □
4. _____	Classroom behavior
5. _____	Comportamiento en la clase □ □
6. _____	Playground behavior
7. _____	Comportamiento en la yarda □ □
8. _____	Homework
9. _____	Tarea □ □
10. _____	Work quality
11. _____	Cualidad de trabajo □ □
12. _____	Spelling _____%
13. _____	Deletreo □ □
14. _____	Math _____%
15. _____	Matemática □ □
16. _____	Comments Comentario
17. _____	_____
18. _____	
19. _____	Parent's signature Firma del padre
20. _____	

See the back of this sheet for sentence dictation.

The Organized Teacher's Guide to Your First Year of Teaching — CD 72   © The McGraw-Hill Companies, Inc.

72
Weekly Assessment 2
(for upper grades)

Name _____
Date _____

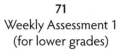

List all daily assignments below. Complete each day's assignments and return this sheet, signed by a parent, the next morning.

Weekly Spelling List	Daily Assignments
1. _____	Monday _____
2. _____	_____
3. _____	Parent's signature _____
4. _____	Tuesday _____
5. _____	_____
6. _____	Parent's signature _____
7. _____	Wednesday _____
8. _____	_____
9. _____	Parent's signature _____
10. _____	Thursday _____
Bonus _____	_____
	Parent's signature _____
	Friday _____
	_____
	Parent's signature _____

The Organized Teacher's Guide to Your First Year of Teaching — CD 73   © The McGraw-Hill Companies, Inc.

73 🖥
Weekly Homework 1
(for lower grades)

Name _____   Date _____

List all daily assignments below. Complete each day's assignments and return this sheet, signed by a parent, the next morning.

Weekly Spelling List	Daily Assignments
1. _____	Monday _____
2. _____	_____
3. _____	_____
4. _____	Parent's signature _____
5. _____	Tuesday _____
6. _____	_____
7. _____	_____
8. _____	Parent's signature _____
9. _____	Wednesday _____
10. _____	_____
11. _____	_____
12. _____	Parent's signature _____
13. _____	Thursday _____
14. _____	_____
15. _____	_____
16. _____	Parent's signature _____
17. _____	Friday _____
18. _____	_____
19. _____	_____
20. _____	Parent's signature _____
Bonus _____	

The Organized Teacher's Guide to Your First Year of Teaching — CD 74   © The McGraw-Hill Companies, Inc.

74 🖥
Weekly Homework 2
(for upper grades)

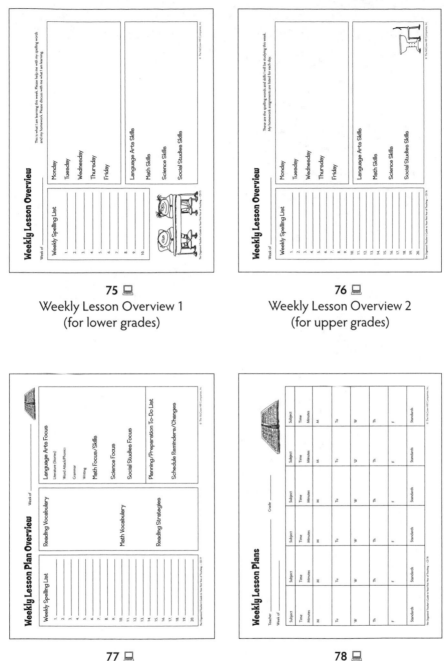

75 🖳
Weekly Lesson Overview 1
(for lower grades)

76 🖳
Weekly Lesson Overview 2
(for upper grades)

77 🖳
Weekly Lesson Plan Overview

78 🖳
Weekly Lesson Plans

Welcome Back!

To Parents and Guardians:

Welcome back to school. I am pleased to have your child in my class and am looking forward to a productive, fun-filled year.

I would like to invite you to visit my website at

http://teacherweb.com/CA/TexasElementary/MathewJackson/

Every week, I update the website with a list of homework, spelling and vocabulary words, upcoming assemblies and/or field trips, classroom requirements, and a list of books that I think students might enjoy reading. I often post blogs on the website, where parents can chime in and share ideas, experiences, and thoughts about the concepts we are studying. This is also a good place to communicate with me.

In addition to the website, I will send home a weekly newsletter, along with your child's spelling test. The sheet with the spelling test includes a progress report and test scores for the week. Please sign the sheet and return it the next day. There is a Comments section, which you can use to write me a note if you have a question or concern that I should address.

I intend to be easily accessible and will respond to your child's needs as much as possible. I want all of us to enjoy the year and learn a lot.

I look forward to meeting you, so please come by and introduce yourself before or after school.

In the meantime, feel free to e-mail me or call me at the school.

Mr. Jackson – Room 4
jjackson@maudlin.com
323-555-7788 (school phone number)

79
Welcome Letter
(sample)

Welcome Back!

79 🖥️
Welcome Letter
(blank)

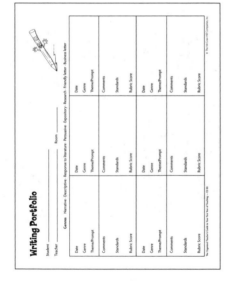

80 🖥️
Writing Portfolio

INDEX

CD templates are indicated in CAPITAL AND SMALL CAPITAL LETTERS; *template numbers are in square brackets.*